Woodrow

Wilson

Biography

The Visionary Who Shaped Modern America

CHERLYSSA HOOPER

Table of Content

Part I: Long Past Due
Chapter 1: Kindred Causes

Hundreds of years ago, when Woodrow Wilson's ancestors lived and died in Scotland, Ireland, and England, and the American democratic experiment was just getting started, men and women debated, as they do today, the practical application of Enlightenment principles of humanity, liberty, and equality under the law. Even when men dominated women and fellow humans were slaves because of their race, the principles made no distinction between race and gender.

From the beginning, the drives for abolition and women's rights stemmed from shared ideas. The movements advanced concurrently and had many of the same leaders. Propertied women were eligible to vote even before the Declaration of Independence, according to the statutes of the majority of colonial governments. Residents of the Quaker colony of Pennsylvania petitioned against slavery in 1688, seven years after its creation. All humans have inherent rights that should not be denied.

Beginning in 1763, Quakers in America barred anyone involved in slavery from membership. In 1773, Virginia's slaveholding Patrick Henry said that he praised the Quakers "for their noble effort to abolish slavery," which was "equally calculated to promote moral and public good."

In 1824, at Monticello, a young but resolute Frances Wright—an embodiment of women's civic and social equality—shared her ideas for abolishing slavery with Jefferson and the Marquis de Lafayette. Elizabeth Cady Stanton, Susan B. Anthony, and Matilda Joslyn Gage chose her portrait as the frontispiece for the first edition of their History of Woman Suffrage. In the years that followed, Wright spoke in front of thousands of people across the country to advocate for equal rights for women.

During his successful candidacy for the Illinois House of Representatives in 1836, Abraham Lincoln advocated for women's suffrage on the condition that they pay taxes or bear arms. "I go for all sharing the privileges of the Government who assist in bearing its burdens," he stated, "by no means excluding women." The Sangamon Journal published the campaign's written pledge. In their history of the time, Anthony and Ida Husted Harper lauded Lincoln for "publicly and unequivocally" supporting women's voting rights. Lincoln's "later utterances," they added, "indicated that he did not change his position."

Douglass agreed with Stanton, claiming that "the power to choose rulers and make laws [is] the right by which all others [are] secured." He most certainly repeated his convention remarks in an editorial published the following week in his newspaper, the North Star. "[I]n terms of political rights," he reasoned, "we believe that women are justly entitled to everything we claim for men." We go on to say that we believe that all political rights that are beneficial to men are also beneficial to women. Douglass argued that women have the same intelligence and accountability as men, and that if the government is just and based on consent, there is no reason to deny them the right to vote or participate in making and enforcing laws.

One year after the Seneca Falls convention, Lucretia Mott took a break from giving speeches to attend a lecture on women in Shakespeare's works. She might have been expecting a pleasant diversion. But the guy at the lectern, Boston's Richard Henry Dana Sr., was more than just a history buff. Born in the previous century and now sixty-two years old, his opinion of women's proper roles differed little from the present day and Elizabethan times.

He said the woman's position had been determined by "God's ordaining." He appeared to be unaware of the changes that had transpired during his lifetime, as women were now taking their positions in education, the arts and sciences, and public policy discussions like abolition and temperance. Dana said allowing women to vote would disrupt family life and leave America "homeless." In what would become a cliche among opponents of the suffrage campaign in the decades to come, he defined women's "distinct attributes" as follows:

Mott's "Discourse on Woman," delivered on a chilly evening one week before Christmas 1849, went beyond refuting Dana's romantic assertions about human beings to make a positive case for women's liberty as a necessary extension of the Enlightenment ideals on which the United States was founded. She adopted a cautious approach to the matter, attempting to persuade rather than offend her audience. She did not argue against marriage, but rather for one in which "the independence of the husband and wife will be equal, their dependence mutual, and their obligations reciprocal." It was absolutely OK, she maintained, to be "womanly" and "dignified," but she warned against "effeminacy" and encouraged women, like men, to exercise and develop their inherent physical power. Above all, a woman should not be hesitant to "exercise her reason, and her noblest powers."

Of course, Mott's very appearance onstage in Philadelphia vividly demonstrated that women were not only already reformers, but also at the forefront of the abolitionist struggle.

In the years leading up to the Civil War, the abolition and suffrage movements grew in strength, sometimes concurrently, sometimes in conflict. Both challenged accepted views of who is a full citizen. Both profited from their interaction. Abolition progressed due to women's speaking, organizing, and lobbying, and the fact that they were doing so helped women overcome traditional barriers to political participation. There is no better example of this than how women's movement leaders rallied around the cause when Congress threatened to repeal the restriction on slavery in the territories in 1854.

Senator Stephen Douglas of Illinois introduced the Kansas-Nebraska measure, which posed a threat. It intended to invalidate the long-standing Missouri Compromise, allowing slavery to be practiced throughout the remaining Louisiana Territory. Its defining characteristic was "popular sovereignty," which allowed Congress to delegate the issue of slavery to local governments. Plebiscites in the sparsely populated new territories of Kansas and Nebraska would decide whether persons may be considered property. Few in the abolitionist camp thought that Missouri slaveholders would send thousands of mercenaries across the Kansas border, clog the voting boxes, and quickly pass pro-slavery legislation.

With Smith's help, Anthony drew no fewer than 76 members of Congress to an evening speech on abolition and women's rights given by her colleague and traveling companion, the famed lecturer Ernestine Rose. Buoyed by his accomplishment, Anthony met with the Speaker of the House, Kentucky Democrat Linn Boyd, a slave owner who was devoted to passing the Kansas-Nebraska measure. She requested that he utilize the Capitol as a platform to speak out against the legislation in question. She also desired the "Capitol Hall," as the House chamber was originally known. Undoubtedly caught aback by her audacious plea, the Speaker turned her down. He said it was "a standing [policy] to allow no one to speak there on any subject."

Anthony left the conference dejected. Shortly after, while listening to the House floor debate on the Kansas-Nebraska bill, she was particularly outraged that the bill's advocates claimed to be making a moral case for enslaving humans. "How hateful is slavery," she wrote in her diary, "that it prostrates such nobility of soul to such base ends."

After the majority of northern Democrats in the House voted with their southern counterparts to pass the Kansas-Nebraska measure in late May, the Republican movement grew rapidly. Outraged by the prospect of imposing slavery on the North, dissident Democrats, "Conscience" Whigs, and Free Soilers from every northern state gathered together in an attempt to form their own state Republican organizations in time for the November elections. This new party's midwives included well-known men like Salmon Chase, Benjamin Wade, and Joshua Giddings from Ohio, William Seward and Horace Greeley from New York, George Julian from Indiana, and Charles Sumner from Massachusetts. However, without the decades of groundbreaking work by abolitionist women that had preceded this moment—their petitions to Congress and testimony before state legislatures, their published tracts, and their platform lectures—it is unlikely that any antislavery party could have coalesced so quickly.

As the March 1855 territorial election approached, Missouri's slave-owning U.S. senator David Atchison, whose tenure in Congress had just expired, assisted in leading 5,000 men across the boundary. These "border ruffians" spread out far and wide to frighten election judges, seize polling locations at force, and cast illicit ballots. They did not even attempt to stake a claim for land to establish "actual residence" before voting, as required by law. The election results offered conclusive evidence of fraud. The pre-election census in Kansas revealed 2,905 eligible voters, but 6,307 ballots were cast. When the dust settled, pro-slavery factions claimed they had won 92% of the seats in the new legislature.

Susan Anthony's personal interest in this increasingly violent fight had grown to include her brother Merritt, who had only a year prior been filling envelopes for her statewide women's rights petition drive. After traveling across the country by train, boat, horse-drawn wagon, and his own legs, he arrived in the heart of a conflict zone. While his older sister worried for his safety, she tried to help from afar by working for the Republican Party in New York. However, she felt severely limited by her inability to vote. If she had been born a man, she said after attending her first Republican gathering in 1855, "I doubt I would be an active, zealous advocate of Republicanism." She despised being outside, watching. Thousands of other women must have felt the same way. Women accounted for about half of Republican meeting attendance in the 1850s.

By 1856, Kansas Territory's lawlessness and brutality, all in the cause of preserving slavery, had become a national embarrassment. In a report delivered aloud to the United States Senate, a Kansas priest recounted what life was like in Kansas for those who opposed slavery. "Our citizens have been shot at," according to his testimony, "our houses invaded, hay-ricks burnt, corn and other provisions plundered, cattle driven off, all communication cut off between us and the States, wagons on the way to us with provisions stopped and plundered, and the drivers taken prisoners."

While Atchison and Sheriff Samuel Jones prepared to unleash their man-made storm that would demolish Lawrence—the Saturday Evening Post dubbed it a "monster posse"—Charles Sumner took to the Senate floor to condemn the violence and to shame his colleagues who supported slavery for their role in it.

His address praised the selflessness of women fighting slavery in Kansas. He compared them to the "matrons of Rome who poured their jewels into the treasury for the public defense." Compared to "the wives of Prussia, who, with delicate fingers, clothed their defenders against French invasion," the courageous ladies of Kansas reminded me of "the mothers of our own Revolution, who sent forth their sons, covered over with prayers and blessings, to combat for human rights." He claimed that the ladies of the 1776 Revolutionary War "did nothing of self-sacrifice truer than did these women on this occasion."

Women in Kansas served as scouts and guards for the Free State militia, practiced marksmanship to help repel "border ruffians," smuggled ammunition from Missouri under their skirts, manufactured cartridges for rifles used to defend Lawrence, drove buggies carrying hundreds of pounds of supplies, and rode into hostile territory to serve as spies. When their dwellings were attacked, they were known to pour hot water at the perpetrators. In more emergency situations, they may shoot on sight. One Lawrence woman threatened to shoot the notorious pro-slavery sheriff Samuel Jones if he attempted to arrest her husband. The sheriff backed down, apparently saying, "I'd rather face an army of men than one furious woman."

Sumner was chastised by Democratic senators and the press from the minute he took his place on the Senate floor at the end of his two-day address. The Alexandria Gazette criticized him for his "disposition," noting that he addressed the leaders of the Senate's massive pro-slavery caucus by name. Sumner had tried, in flamboyant fashion, to make them appear ridiculous. He mocked South Carolina's Andrew Butler's "chivalry" by comparing him to Don Quixote, a knight-errant heroically protecting the "harlot, Slavery," and presented Stephen Douglas as an obsequious Sancho Panza assisting in the immoral quest. In stark contrast to the virtuous ladies of Lawrence who were supporting freedom, Sumner denounced Butler's obsession with slavery—the "mistress to whom he has made his vows," even though she is "ugly to others."

The official discussion record for May 20, 1856, contains no information regarding the stench in the room, but the comments that followed were caustic. Lewis Cass, a Democrat from Michigan who would soon become secretary of state in James Buchanan's new pro-slavery cabinet, got to his feet as Sumner finished. The lengthy oration had allowed him nearly 24 hours to think of a good retort. "Such a speech," Cass began, conjuring all the indignity he could muster, was "the most un-American and unpatriotic that ever grated on the ears of the members of this high body."

However, it was the neatly printed word, not the bawdy spectacle of the live event, that conveyed the message of "The Crime Against Kansas" across the country. Sumner had arranged for the complete text of the address to be printed ahead of time, but he still struggled to keep up with requests from people for copies. His own efforts were surpassed by popular reprints that appeared apparently everywhere suddenly.

Sumner's concentration was broken by the faint sound of adjacent footfalls, which alerted him to the intruder's existence. He looked up from his papers as a guy loomed above him, partially blocking the light from the enormous brass chandelier above, while shafts of the springtime sun glinted periodically through the circle of skylights, casting sparkling reflections on his mahogany desk. He did not recognize the assailant or his two accomplices, although all three were Democratic House members. Preston Brooks of South Carolina confronted Sumner with a gold-capped walking staff as hard as whalebone, which he had specifically chosen to bludgeon him. One of the conspirators, Virginia's Henry Edmundson, had previously been jailed by the House sergeant at arms for attempting to assault an Ohio congressman and was armed with a loaded gun.

The senator heard a harsh snap as the weapon ripped through his flesh and crashed into his scalp, compressing his brain with hundreds of pounds of force in milliseconds. Sumner lost his sight almost immediately, as the severe impact most likely caused a brain contusion and internal bleeding swollen the visual cortex. However, his torment was only beginning.

The frenetic violence continued until the outraged congressman, six foot one and muscular, smashed the end of his walking stick on Sumner's head as he lay motionless on the Senate floor. The remaining two-foot piece of wood in Brooks' palm proved to be an equally powerful weapon, with sharp splintered ends functioning as a scourge. He kept pounding Sumner's head "as hard as he could," according to a witness, who described how the blows "made a good deal more noise after the stick was broken."

A fellow senator tried to save Sumner, saying, "Don't kill him!" However, one of the conspirators stepped forward, swinging his own cane above his head and yelling, "Let them alone, God damn you!" Sumner now appeared completely asleep, yet the relentless pummeling continued. "Brooks kept up his blows with great rapidity," one of the senators claimed, "until Mr. Sumner sank to the floor." Sumner's arms and shoulders became black.

And then it ended.

Sumner was in serious condition for several days and may have died due to head injuries sustained from twenty or thirty hits. Cornelius

Boyle, the doctor who treated Sumner on the afternoon of the assault, told two other witnesses that the skull wounds were "the worst wounds of the kind he had ever seen," and that they were so deep that "he would have sworn before a court that it was done with a brick." Sumner's psychological and physical disabilities were severe enough to prevent him from returning to his Senate duties for more than three years.

The attack on Charles Sumner, a Harvard lawyer and prominent abolitionist who would lead the nascent Republican Party, was designed to send a message to anybody who opposed legally protected slavery. However, rather than scaring the antislavery movement or Sumner himself, it inflamed sentiment on both sides of the debate, surprisingly influencing another emerging drama: the fight for women's voting rights.

Chapter 2: Woodrows and Wilsons

Woodrow Wilson was born in Staunton, Virginia, December 28, 1856. It was the year of "Bleeding Kansas" and the Capitol attack on Charles Sumner, Dred Scott's case reached the Supreme Court, pro-slavery Democrat James Buchanan was elected president, and Lucy Stone presided over the seventh national Woman's Rights Convention in New York City.

The United States in the 1850s was rife with controversy, requiring individuals, including the future president's parents, to choose sides on a slew of deeply divided issues in politics, religion, culture, and even science. The problems were as vast as they were intractable. Slavery, of course. As early as 1851, in the Wilsons' second year of marriage— seven years before Lincoln's "House Divided" speech at the Illinois Republican Convention—it was clear enough even for Victor Hugo thousands of miles across the Atlantic that the "United States must renounce slavery, or they must renounce liberty." Before the end of the decade, while Woodrow Wilson was still a kid, John Brown was hanged for murder, treason, and inciting an uprising, the clearest indication yet that civil war was on the way.

Joseph Wilson was born and raised in Steubenville, Ohio, where he met Jessie Woodrow, whose Scottish family relocated to Ohio from eastern Ontario when she was six years old. He married Jessie in 1849 in her birthplace of Chillicothe. They married in the same year that Abraham Lincoln, a freshman congressman from Illinois, introduced legislation to abolish slavery in the District of Columbia, which was then under direct congressional authority.

The Wilsons migrated to Virginia in 1851, shortly after the birth of their first child, a daughter called Marion, which at the time had the highest number of enslaved adults and children of any state. It was the family's second move in two short years of marriage. Joseph's meager salaries as a pastor to minuscule audiences were further strained when the Wilsons' daughter Annie was born in 1853, forcing him to supplement his intermittent preaching with tutoring. However, during the family's fourth year in Virginia, Reverend Wilson was able to secure his first lucrative ministry in the Shenandoah Valley town of

Staunton. His spiritual calling now provided abundant material benefits: a handsome salary, a spacious three-story Greek Revival manse on one of the city's most beautiful lots (reputed to be "the best house in Staunton"), and enslaved Black servants to do the Wilsons' laundry, cook their meals, and keep their home clean.

On the third day of Christmas in 1856, Jessie Wilson gave birth to the first of the couple's two sons. He would be named Thomas Woodrow, after Jessie's father and brother.

Tommy Wilson's father delivered a sermon against slavery shortly after Lincoln's election, three months before Fort Sumter, and had it published because he considered it was so important. Reverend Wilson told his segregated First Presbyterian Church congregation— whites in the main pews, enslaved Black people, including the Wilson family servants on the balcony—that "the Bible brings human slavery underneath the sanction of divine authority." He argued that slavery was not only not evil, but also something to "cherish" because it enriched the "superior race" while "saving a lower race." In a note explaining why he was publishing this lecture, Wilson's father expressed his hope that it "may be the means of doing a service to my slaveholding brethren." It was time, he declared, "to meet the infidel fanaticism of our infatuated enemies upon the elevated ground of a divine warrant." God would be on their side in the fight to preserve slavery.

During the Civil War, Reverend Wilson volunteered as a military chaplain in the Confederate army, granting him the status of a staff officer. He also joined the Confederate home defense unit, the Silver Greys. He utilized his church as a hospital for Confederate soldiers, and an internment camp. Union prisoners of war were held hostage in a stockade until they could be transferred to Andersonville Prison, which is still notorious in the twenty-first century for its wartime horrors.

Tommy Wilson's father articulated his views on the role of women with the same religious zeal that he used to defend slavery. Reverend Wilson stated in another sermon deemed suitable for publishing that a woman's "physically weak nature" required her to submit to men. Her allotted location was the home, with the male "ruling at the head" and the woman "subject to that head." Women, he claimed, must stay "away from the rush and storm of life," because their inherently "soft voice" is "less obtrusive"—suited not for "crowded assemblies" but rather "the little meetings of the family." He hurried to clarify that women should not regard this as a mark of inferiority. He said a woman's position is just as vital as a man's, but in different ways. A woman's specific obligations include promoting religion inside her family, since religion is her "peculiar ornament" and "the right foundation of her peculiar influence." Wilson's father told her that she should have an education, but it shouldn't be the same as a man's. Women's education should center on "religious training" that is "connected with their families" so that they can take responsibility for "the future of their children."

Wartime reality bears little resemblance to Reverend Joseph Wilson's concept of women limiting themselves to "little meetings of the family." Most American women didn't respond to his depiction of a "physically weak nature." In their History of Woman Suffrage, Elizabeth Cady Stanton, Susan B. Anthony, and Matilda Joslyn Gage describe how even the most "delicate, refined women, unused to care and toil" were abruptly driven into manual labor. Millions of women served in the conflict. Women held one-third of all manufacturing employment. Their responsibilities included making uniforms (shirts, pants, socks, shoes, outerwear) and equipment such as knapsacks, haversacks, and tents, and leather cartridge cases, bayonet scabbards, and belt sets. Women were also employed in cartridge factories, and their jobs may be hazardous. Scores of women were killed in industrial accidents, and many more were burned and injured when ammunition exploded in arsenals in the District of Columbia, Jackson, and Richmond.

Women on both sides of the war gathered battlefield intelligence, conducted reconnaissance, and engaged in espionage, including the formerly enslaved Harriet Tubman, who helped the Union army as a scout and spy. Women provided emergency care on and off the battlefield. At least 400 women disguised themselves as men and served as soldiers, some of them died in action.

Necessity prompted millions of women to take over jobs previously held by drafted males. Instead of conventional home chores, women were responsible for planting and harvesting crops, working in mills and factories, managing retail outlets, and performing secretarial labor to support every facet of American society at the time.

The war spurred more women to take the stage as political speakers. Only a decade previously, the Speaker of the House responded with surprise before refusing Susan B. Anthony's request to talk at the Capitol. In 1864, the Speaker of the House and the President of the Senate formally invited a woman to speak there. Over 100 congressmen signed Anna Dickinson's invitation. President and Mrs. Lincoln, and cabinet ministers, were among the dignitaries who attended her speech in a packed House chamber.

Across the Atlantic, the London Daily Telegraph couldn't "imagine the British House of Commons granting the use of their hall and the honours of the Speaker's chair" to a woman. The young Dickinson's impassioned public speeches in defense of the Union drew large crowds not only in Washington but throughout the North. She collaborated with the now-famous Frederick Douglass during a huge meeting in Philadelphia's National Hall to urge African American recruitment. She was a generation younger than her pals Anthony and Stanton, and only fourteen years older than Tommy Wilson. She eventually used the same speaker's bureau as Mark Twain, commanding four times his speaking fees.

On January 31, 1865, Congress passed what became known as the 13th Amendment, which prohibited slavery. The war had not yet ended; Sherman's march into Georgia, while sparing Tommy's Augusta, was a recent memory. The state's reaction to the new amendment was expected. The Macon Telegraph slammed it for "degrading the master" and "putting him on the same level as his former slave."

Within six months, their organization had expanded to over 5,000 members who collected signatures on petitions to Congress from all 50 states. Charles Sumner, an associate of the League, soon took the petitions to the Senate, where he convened a select committee to discuss "all propositions... concerning slavery and the treatment of freedmen." By April 1864, Stanton and Anthony had buried the Senate with petitions signed by a quarter-million people.

That same month, a two-thirds Senate majority approved Lincoln's proposed amendment to the Constitution. The League then increased its signature gathering efforts, putting more pressure on the House of Representatives. By August, they had over 400,000 signatures, with women accounting for two-thirds of the total. After previously rejecting the abolition amendment, the House of Representatives added its vote of support on January 31, 1865, with women, led by Stanton and Anthony, playing a crucial part in the final chapter of slavery.

When Lee came to Augusta later in Tommy's adolescence, the young man made his way to the front of the crowd, near enough to look into Lee's eyes. He was in amazement. In a speech at the University of North Carolina near the end of his tenure as president of Princeton, he made it apparent that his hero worship of Lee had not waned after four decades. Lee was a "great man," a "hero," and a "ideal" to him, and he strove to help others "by the power of love." His childhood brush with Lee, he claimed, had put him "in the presence of consuming force."

Tommy Wilson's home state approved the 13th Amendment on December 6, 1865, as required for re-entry into the Union. As the last of the twenty-seven states to ratify, Georgia essentially included abolition into the Constitution. It was not a distinction the state sought. "The country filled with vagrants," Wilson grumbled of the amendment's effects, writing from Princeton two generations later.

Worse, in his opinion, was the Republican proposal to make vagrants voters. As he stated in his History of the American People, the men in Congress intended to accomplish this by another constitutional amendment. The ultimate goal, Wilson stated, was to "place the negroes on a footing of civil equality with the whites in the South" in a fashion that would be "unalterable" if Democrats from the former Confederacy were readmitted to Congress.

Wilson, writing in the early twentieth century, chastised Senator Charles Sumner for claiming that "the cause of human rights and the Union needed the ballots as well as the muskets of the colored men." Sumner, he argued, was a mere "party politician" who backed voting rights for freed slaves because of a desire for "complete power" over the Democrats. Wilson levied the same claim against Illinois

Representative Thaddeus Stevens, a strong abolitionist in the House. He accused Stevens of being "callous" to southern interests, describing him as a partisan whose primary goal was to protect the Republican majority.

Of course, the women's suffrage movement had been working for nearly a generation to make universal suffrage a reality. This made them passionate proponents of the proposed 14th Amendment—or, at the very least, its basic draft. However, many of them quickly abandoned their support for reasons that contradicted Wilson's criticisms. Their issue was that the proposed phrase barred voting rights discrimination against a state's "male inhabitants," but did not address discrimination against women. If this wording is adopted into the Constitution, it will be the first time in the nation's history that constitutional protection is provided to males rather than females.

Elizabeth Cady Stanton quickly grasped the gravity of the situation. "If that word 'male' be inserted," she wrote to her cousin Gerrit Smith, "it will take us a century to get it out." She and Susan B. Anthony went into action, hoping to repeat their 13th Amendment victory. They planned a nationwide petition drive for a constitutional amendment adopting universal suffrage, expecting to once again put overwhelming public pressure on Congress. But this time, they went further. They concluded that until the new amendment provided voting rights protections to women and Black men, they would fight against it, arguing that women needed the vote more than Black males and should be prioritized.

This was a dangerous plan. If Congress passed the 14th Amendment without the required adjustment, Anthony, Stanton, and anybody else in the women's suffrage movement who supported them would be forced to oppose the ratification of many key civil rights achievements. Even without women's suffrage, the 14th Amendment would overturn the Dred Scott ruling, which portrayed Black people as "beings of an inferior order," with "no rights the white man is bound to respect." It would nullify the infamous three-fifths clause. It would also include new constitutional protections of due process and equal protection under the law—reforms that would apply to both men and women.

On May 10, 1866, the 14th Amendment passed the House of Representatives, but the offensive word "male" was still included. Thaddeus Stevens, co-chair of the bipartisan committee writing the amendment, advocated for gender-neutral language. In reality, the joint committee's original proposed version mentioned "persons," for which Stanton credited Stevens. On the House floor, Stevens defended his sex-neutral wording. "I certainly shall never vote to insert the word 'male' or the word 'white' in the national Constitution," he continued at the time.

However, his strategy was unsuccessful. A Democratic member of the committee reportedly opposed, saying it "would enfranchise all the Southern wenches." A Republican colleague on the committee maintained that "suffrage for black men will be all the strain the Republican Party can withstand." Members of the New York, Illinois, and Indiana delegations put additional pressure on the committee to strike the sex-neutral language. They understood that if Stevens was successful in using the phrase "persons," the 14th Amendment would go a long way toward enfranchising the country's women, since any state that continued to deny women the right to vote risked losing representation in Congress.

With supermajorities required to adopt an amendment, even Anthony and Stanton's longstanding ally Charles Sumner, who faithfully brought their petitions to the Senate throughout the debate, has declined to support the proposition just now. He was concerned that the added weight of women's suffrage would give uncertain members one more reason to vote against the amendment. This irritated Stanton and Anthony beyond measure. "Even Charles Sumner bends to the spirit of compromise," Anthony wrote in her diary.

For the next year, when the Senate discussed the 14th Amendment, the new organization fought to remove the word "male" from the document. However, the Senate and House eventually reached an agreement on compromise language that retained the section about male citizens intact, and the amendment was sent to the states for ratification in June 1866. It was incorporated into the Constitution two summers later, in July 1868. In a sad irony, the amendment that removed the last vestiges of the founders' original text also served as an opportunity for the new framers of the mid-nineteenth century to institutionalize another form of legal and social bias, this time against women.

Wilson's History of the American People described the 14th Amendment's amazing journey as a scandal. But not because women were denied equal treatment under the law—he wrote nothing about that. Rather, in the presidential election of 1868, which followed the ratification of the 14th Amendment, the votes of the southern states "were turned over to the Republican candidate, as expected, by the negro voters."

Chapter 3: Bittersweet at Princeton

Tommy Wilson was not far from home attending the College of New Jersey. The trip to Princeton was just about 200 miles longer than his previous move from Augusta to Wilmington, and it was much easier by train. His new school's emphasis on Presbyterian beliefs was also pleasant, as it provided a familiar rhythm to his schedule right away. Religious teaching was required not only on Sundays, but throughout the week. The Presbyterian minister who functioned as the college's president recited the Bible, there were mandated student-led prayer groups twice a week, voluntary prayer gatherings every night, and guest ministers preached on campus in between.

Wilson, like Davidson, was not a standout student at the College of New Jersey, and he was never named one of the "honor men." According to historian Henry Bragdon, the fact that the college was not intellectually difficult at the time—"more like a preparatory school than a university," demonstrates that his concerns were elsewhere. Wilson wrote for the student newspaper, sang in the glee club, was the baseball team's student manager, and belonged to the debate club in Whig Hall, one of two societies that separated the student population. In addition, he joined an unauthorized student organization with seventeen of his North Carolina peers. They dubbed themselves, unoriginally, the "Tar Heels," and offered each other shelter from the northerners' toxic ideas on secession, race, and the wisdom of reconstruction.

Tommy was deeply immersed in politics and administration by the fall of his second year at Princeton, following a summer in North Carolina where he studied about the prominent slaveholders John C. Calhoun and Henry Clay. He had also become a staunch Democratic supporter. According to William Bayard Hale's 1912 campaign biography, Wilson "was known as a Democrat of stout opinions from the day he first opened his mouth on campus."

Trescot wrote a lengthy piece immediately before the 1876 presidential election in which he praised Lucius Quintus Cincinnatus Lamar, a Confederate appointment. (President Grover Cleveland eventually appointed Lamar to the Supreme Court, where he defended racial segregation in the classic case of Plessy v. Ferguson.) Lamar, a Democratic member of Congress from Mississippi known for defending Klansmen prosecuted under the Ku Klux Klan Act, blamed the South's postwar troubles solely on the fact that Black men were allowed to vote. Trescot, in turn, praised Congressman Lamar's intentions to suppress votes. Trescot believed it was desirable if "the negro…will be reduced to a position of inferior influence" to the "natural intelligence and culture" of white men.

Wilson believed that Reconstruction was illegitimate, as did the Republicans who authored it. In his diary, he criticized Governor Hayes as "that weak instrument of the corrupt Republicans." A few days later, he lamented Robert E. Lee's prelapsarian days, exclaiming, "Lee is one of my favorites."

Wilson could easily join his fellow Tar Heels in a scathing criticism of the Republicans and their candidate who backed Black suffrage. However, he struggled to communicate these ideas to the rest of his classmates outside his ideological bubble. In response to Tommy's complaints about those "ignorant" classmates fascinated with Hayes, his mother stated her fear that "their offensive sayings" and "insolence would drag him into a fight." She was concerned that he may be wounded and warned him to stop talking "about knocking anybody down." According to his own account, Wilson grew "white with rage" when other Princeton men defended Reconstruction. But, following his mother's advice, instead of arguing, he walked away angrily, saying over his shoulder, "You don't know what you're talking about!"

As a New York Democratic convention delegate, Tilden voted against equal suffrage for Black Americans and in favor of strict property requirements for voting. He opposed the Emancipation Proclamation, Lincoln's military goals that extended beyond the Union, and slaveholders' rights to security for their human "property" throughout the Civil military. As chairman of the New York Democratic Party Committee throughout Reconstruction (and chairman of Seymour's presidential campaign), he denounced the Republican policy of "meddling with everything [in] the reconstructed Southern States," calling it "the scandal and shame of the country." Following the war, he opposed the 15th Amendment, Black suffrage in the South, and the

Freedmen's Bureau.

Wilson's views on universal suffrage hardened as he reached his senior year of college. His third-year article had at least acknowledged the idea that with enough education, "the masses" might ultimately consider it "a blessing." He refused to participate in a discussion since he was assigned to speak in favor of universal suffrage, albeit merely for academic purposes. He did not want to appear in public defending the idea. He made this decision with encouragement from both sides of his family. "Either a limitation of suffrage," Joseph Wilson warned his son at the time, or America will have "anarchy in twenty-five years or sooner." Tommy's mother told him she was proud of his decision. "I was sorry you could not enter" the competition, his mother wrote when he pulled out of the debate, but by asking him to make the argument for weakening white men's voting strength, "they chose a question that made it impossible." His friend Charles Talcott offered him moral support, saying, "You were right in staying out: arguing against settled convictions, in my opinion, injures a man more than it benefits him."

Wilson's major success at the College of New Jersey occurred in his fourth and final year. It was a typed, double-spaced, 25-page essay on Congress that was eventually published in the International Review, a respected political journal. Although he was a 22-year-old student who had never visited the House or Senate, he boldly professed understanding of what was fundamentally wrong with those institutions' inner workings. His unwavering confidence persuaded both his twenty-something editor (ironically, his future Senate antagonist, Henry Cabot Lodge) and the magazine's readers that he should be taken seriously.

Wilson recognized that this unprecedented revision of the Constitution would raise concerns about "too much authority, too complete control, placed within the reach of the central government." However, he argued it would cause better transparency. "Executive departments," he claimed, "keep all of their operations under a constant stream of daylight," but congressional "committees do everything in the dark." This patently untrue assertion revealed Wilson's ignorance of the activities of both the British and American administrations at the time.

In both countries, executive departments frequently conducted business in private and kept many secrets. They still do. More fundamentally, his essay was not informed by any first hand investigation of the actual procedures of congressional committees at the time. Wilson paid no attention to how the specialized committee structure could be very responsive to emerging currents of public opinion, or how much committee work was done in public, rather than in secret.

Even years later, when he was president of Princeton University, Wilson stuck to the views he first presented in "Cabinet Government." He elaborated on these in Constitutional Government in the United States, an anthology of eight of his speeches released in 1908. Constitutional Government echoes Wilson's three-decade-old claim that the institutional checks and balances on the president are the main weakness of the American constitutional system. Wilson argued that the executive's involvement in lawmaking should extend far beyond just vetoing bad legislation. The president should "be given an opportunity to make good ones." Furthermore, the president should be "the leader of his party and the guide of the nation." While lamenting that the Constitution does not describe these functions, Wilson went on to suggest that a successful, activist president should not let a "mechanical theory" of the Constitution's constraints on executive power get in the way.

Wilson's contrarian prescription for a legislative branch more accountable to the presidency, first conceived at the College of New Jersey and later developed throughout his academic career, was unquestionably based on his personal experience with a domineering Republican Congress that had waged war on the South and imposed a dozen years of Reconstruction afterward. His desire to subordinate Congress to presidential authority was inextricably linked to his belief in white male superiority and his opposition to universal suffrage. It is not surprising, therefore, that once southern Democrats regained their pre-Civil War influence in the House and Senate—a development that coincided with his election to the presidency in 1912—he would demurely back away from his earlier attacks on the separation of powers in the Constitution. His beliefs about race and sex, on the other hand, would remain central to his thought for much longer.

On January 11, 1878, in the middle of Tommy Wilson's junior year at the College of New Jersey and one year before he published his paper in the International Review, the Senate Committee on Privileges and Elections held two full days of public hearings on the women's suffrage amendment introduced by California Republican Aaron Sargent the day before. By this point, the man whom the National Woman Suffrage Association dubbed "our champion in the Senate" had become Susan B. Anthony's primary political friend. Senators in the packed hearing chamber heard testimony from over a dozen supporters, including Elizabeth Cady Stanton, Matilda Joslyn Gage, 85-year-old Julia Smith, and even Victor Hugo from across the Atlantic, whose sentiments were presented to the committee. If Wilson had attended the hearings or read about them in the media, the college student who rejected criticism that his idea represented a dangerous centralization of government authority would have had to reconsider his position. Priscilla Rand Lawrence, a Massachusetts witness, told the senators that decades of denying women the opportunity to vote had already resulted in "the power of our government being centralized in the hands of a few."

Tommy Wilson was not far from home attending the College of New Jersey. The trip to Princeton was just about 200 miles longer than his previous move from Augusta to Wilmington, and it was much easier by train. His new school's emphasis on Presbyterian beliefs was also pleasant, as it provided a familiar rhythm to his schedule right away. Religious teaching was required not only on Sundays, but throughout the week. The Presbyterian minister who functioned as the college's president recited the Bible, there were mandated student-led prayer groups twice a week, voluntary prayer gatherings every night, and guest ministers preached on campus in between.

Wilson, like Davidson, was not a standout student at the College of New Jersey, and he was never named one of the "honor men." According to historian Henry Bragdon, the fact that the college was not intellectually difficult at the time—"more like a preparatory school than a university," demonstrates that his concerns were elsewhere. Wilson wrote for the student newspaper, sang in the glee club, was the baseball team's student manager, and belonged to the debate club in Whig Hall, one of two societies that separated the student population.

In addition, he joined an unauthorized student organization with seventeen of his North Carolina peers. They dubbed themselves, unoriginally, the "Tar Heels," and offered each other shelter from the northerners' toxic ideas on secession, race, and the wisdom of reconstruction.

Tommy was deeply immersed in politics and administration by the fall of his second year at Princeton, following a summer in North Carolina where he studied about the prominent slaveholders John C. Calhoun and Henry Clay. He had also become a staunch Democratic supporter. According to William Bayard Hale's 1912 campaign biography, Wilson "was known as a Democrat of stout opinions from the day he first opened his mouth on campus."

Trescot wrote a lengthy piece immediately before the 1876 presidential election in which he praised Lucius Quintus Cincinnatus Lamar, a Confederate appointment. (President Grover Cleveland eventually appointed Lamar to the Supreme Court, where he defended racial segregation in the classic case of Plessy v. Ferguson.) Lamar, a Democratic member of Congress from Mississippi known for defending Klansmen prosecuted under the Ku Klux Klan Act, blamed the South's postwar troubles solely on the fact that Black men were allowed to vote. Trescot, in turn, praised Congressman Lamar's intentions to suppress votes. Trescot believed it was desirable if "the negro...will be reduced to a position of inferior influence" to the "natural intelligence and culture" of white men.

Wilson believed that Reconstruction was illegitimate, as did the Republicans who authored it. In his diary, he criticized Governor Hayes as "that weak instrument of the corrupt Republicans." A few days later, he lamented Robert E. Lee's prelapsarian days, exclaiming, "Lee is one of my favorites."

Wilson could easily join his fellow Tar Heels in a scathing criticism of the Republicans and their candidate who backed Black suffrage. However, he struggled to communicate these ideas to the rest of his classmates outside his ideological bubble. In response to Tommy's complaints about those "ignorant" classmates fascinated with Hayes, his mother stated her fear that "their offensive sayings" and "insolence would drag him into a fight." She was concerned that he may be wounded and warned him to stop talking "about knocking anybody down." According to his own account, Wilson grew "white with rage" when other Princeton men defended Reconstruction. But, following his mother's advice, instead of arguing, he walked away angrily, saying over his shoulder, "You don't know what you're talking about!"

As a New York Democratic convention delegate, Tilden voted against equal suffrage for Black Americans and in favor of strict property requirements for voting. He opposed the Emancipation Proclamation, Lincoln's military goals that extended beyond the Union, and slaveholders' rights to security for their human "property" throughout the Civil military. As chairman of the New York Democratic Party Committee throughout Reconstruction (and chairman of Seymour's presidential campaign), he denounced the Republican policy of "meddling with everything [in] the reconstructed Southern States," calling it "the scandal and shame of the country." Following the war, he opposed the 15th Amendment, Black suffrage in the South, and the Freedmen's Bureau.

Wilson's views on universal suffrage hardened as he reached his senior year of college. His third-year article had at least acknowledged the idea that with enough education, "the masses" might ultimately consider it "a blessing." He refused to participate in a discussion since he was assigned to speak in favor of universal suffrage, albeit merely for academic purposes. He did not want to appear in public defending the idea. He made this decision with encouragement from both sides of his family. "Either a limitation of suffrage," Joseph Wilson warned his son at the time, or America will have "anarchy in twenty-five years or sooner." Tommy's mother told him she was proud of his decision. "I was sorry you could not enter" the competition, his mother wrote when he pulled out of the debate, but by asking him to make the argument for weakening white men's voting strength, "they chose a question that made it impossible." His friend Charles Talcott offered him moral support, saying, "You were right in staying out: arguing against settled convictions, in my opinion, injures a man more than it benefits him."

Wilson's major success at the College of New Jersey occurred in his fourth and final year. It was a typed, double-spaced, 25-page essay on

Congress that was eventually published in the International Review, a respected political journal. Although he was a 22-year-old student who had never visited the House or Senate, he boldly professed understanding of what was fundamentally wrong with those institutions' inner workings. His unwavering confidence persuaded both his twenty-something editor (ironically, his future Senate antagonist, Henry Cabot Lodge) and the magazine's readers that he should be taken seriously.

Wilson recognized that this unprecedented revision of the Constitution would raise concerns about "too much authority, too complete control, placed within the reach of the central government." However, he argued it would cause better transparency. "Executive departments," he claimed, "keep all of their operations under a constant stream of daylight," but congressional "committees do everything in the dark." This patently untrue assertion revealed Wilson's ignorance of the activities of both the British and American administrations at the time. In both countries, executive departments frequently conducted business in private and kept many secrets. They still do. More fundamentally, his essay was not informed by any first hand investigation of the actual procedures of congressional committees at the time. Wilson paid no attention to how the specialized committee structure could be very responsive to emerging currents of public opinion, or how much committee work was done in public, rather than in secret.

Even years later, when he was president of Princeton University, Wilson stuck to the views he first presented in "Cabinet Government." He elaborated on these in Constitutional Government in the United States, an anthology of eight of his speeches released in 1908. Constitutional Government echoes Wilson's three-decade-old claim that the institutional checks and balances on the president are the main weakness of the American constitutional system. Wilson argued that the executive's involvement in lawmaking should extend far beyond just vetoing bad legislation. The president should "be given an opportunity to make good ones." Furthermore, the president should be "the leader of his party and the guide of the nation." While lamenting that the Constitution does not describe these functions, Wilson went on to suggest that a successful, activist president should not let a "mechanical theory" of the Constitution's constraints on executive power get in the way.

Wilson's contrarian prescription for a legislative branch more accountable to the presidency, first conceived at the College of New Jersey and later developed throughout his academic career, was unquestionably based on his personal experience with a domineering Republican Congress that had waged war on the South and imposed a dozen years of Reconstruction afterward. His desire to subordinate Congress to presidential authority was inextricably linked to his belief in white male superiority and his opposition to universal suffrage. It is not surprising, therefore, that once southern Democrats regained their pre-Civil War influence in the House and Senate—a development that coincided with his election to the presidency in 1912—he would demurely back away from his earlier attacks on the separation of powers in the Constitution. His beliefs about race and sex, on the other hand, would remain central to his thought for much longer.

On January 11, 1878, in the middle of Tommy Wilson's junior year at the College of New Jersey and one year before he published his paper in the International Review, the Senate Committee on Privileges and Elections held two full days of public hearings on the women's suffrage amendment introduced by California Republican Aaron Sargent the day before. By this point, the man whom the National Woman Suffrage Association dubbed "our champion in the Senate" had become Susan B. Anthony's primary political friend. Senators in the packed hearing chamber heard testimony from over a dozen supporters, including Elizabeth Cady Stanton, Matilda Joslyn Gage, 85-year-old Julia Smith, and even Victor Hugo from across the Atlantic, whose sentiments were presented to the committee. If Wilson had attended the hearings or read about them in the media, the college student who rejected criticism that his idea represented a dangerous centralization of government authority would have had to reconsider his position. Priscilla Rand Lawrence, a Massachusetts witness, told the senators that decades of denying women the opportunity to vote had already resulted in "the power of our government being centralized in the hands of a few."

Chapter 4: Two Women

During their two-year engagement, which began on September 16, 1883, Woodrow Wilson and Ellen Axson exchanged almost 700 letters. Woodrow in Baltimore was the most regular correspondent, frequently dedicating several pages to himself—his struggles, political ideas, health, insecurities, and desires. Ellen, who was originally from Georgia and later moved to New York City to study at the Art Students League, readily participated in his self-analysis. She supplemented his reflections with her own judgments, prompting him to contemplate deeper. Even the delicate and tolerant bride-to-be warned him against excessive solipsism. "'Know thyself' may be a very good motto," she gently scolded five months into their engagement, "but there are others still better, for instance, 'forget thyself.'"

Shortly before the wedding ceremony, the prospective groom contacted Ellen from Johns Hopkins to express his displeasure with the then-emerging conventional understanding of "a woman's right to lead her own life," as opposed to an existence as an auxiliary to her spouse and children. This claimed "right," he informed her, was a "pernicious falsehood." Granting women the same rights as males would endanger the family as an institution. Worse, it would destroy the foundations of American culture. Wilson insisted that marriage was the "essential condition" for a woman to perform her "proper duties." It was "simply ridiculous" to argue that women "could live exactly the same life that men lead." It was even more unthinkable that a man would assume the duties of the mother and the housekeeper!""This was heresy. "Oh," he moaned, "what a shame to corrupt the truth!"

After virtually exhausting the conceivable slights a man should never have to endure from his wife, Wilson awkwardly added that he was not implying Ellen's cousin was guilty of these transgressions. And he bravely refused to physically threaten a woman. His opposition was founded on chivalry, not on both couples' right to equal respect. He said threatening his wife with a pistol would be cowardly and so unworthy of a man.

This perspective on men's relationships with women reflected the then-prevailing norms of elite southern society—what historian Christopher Lasch later described as "that combination of patriarchal authority and sentimental veneration of women which is the essence of the genteel tradition." It was a tradition idealized in Sir Walter Scott's chivalric novels, which Wilson had read since childhood. Scott's books had a far-reaching impact not only on Wilson but on all of southern white society. Regional authors who largely borrowed from the author's social canon amplified this impact.

In Wilson's chivalric paradigm, women were expected to be obedient so that males could defend the weaker sex. There were jobs for men and women. The latter almost definitely involved housework, preferably with the assistance of slaves. To emphasize this point, Wilson told Ellen about his fury over a recently married Wellesley graduate in his Johns Hopkins rooming house. This woman, he felt it important to inform his fiancée, kept "neither her person nor her room tidy." In Wilson's opinion, this was a grave offense "that will certainly convince her husband of the necessity of a divorce when she undertakes to keep house for him." The fact that the woman was an accomplished scholar, "versed in several languages and on speaking terms with one or two sciences," appears to have counted against her, as it distracted her from housekeeping.

The reviews were divided. Newspapers in New York and San Francisco panned it, as did Harvard's A. Lawrence Lowell, who wrote a lengthy essay in the Atlantic Monthly pointing out various fallacies and errors in analysis. Wilson's plan to graft the primary characteristics of a parliamentary system onto the Constitution, Lowell argued, would be completely impracticable, rendering the presidency and judiciary ineffective and Congress excessively strong. The parliamentary form and the American system of checks and balances both have advantages, he acknowledged, but combining them as Wilson envisioned would cause an out-of-control Frankenstein's monster.

Congressional Government was published in January 1885, but the argument in the popular press continued long into the following year. The dispute undoubtedly benefited the author. Despite his lack of experience, he was suddenly receiving national media coverage as a scholar. Wilson left Johns Hopkins in the summer of 1885, buoyed by the initial public notice and equipped with a teaching offer at Bryn Mawr, a new women's institution near Philadelphia. He was now 28, and Ellen, his fiancée, was 25. He believed it was time he got his first job so they could finally marry.

Fittingly, the June wedding was held in Georgia, where they both grew up. Ellen's parents had both died since she was 21—her mother in 1881 from infection after childbirth, and her father only the previous year, by suicide after a long period of depression—so her grandfather gave her away. Ellen's grandpa, like Woodrow's father, was a Presbyterian clergyman who firmly supported the Confederacy and slavery. The couple honeymooned in the South as well, at the same resort where Woodrow originally introduced Ellen to his family.

Ellen was and will be the type of woman he desired. She shared her husband's ideas about white men's supremacy over all others, and their entitlement to a bigger civic role than all others—including women and herself. However, just as he married Ellen, another lady was about to become the focus of his life. This woman, like Ellen, was intelligent and talented, but she was the complete opposite of Mrs. Wilson. She was a strong supporter of women's political equality, suffrage, and representation in higher education, the professions, and the workplace.

Woodrow Wilson would be terrified of her.

In fact, he was suspicious of the whole idea of women studying the same topics as males. In general, Wilson regarded women's institutions in low regard, and he emphatically opposed the mere concept of any "co-educational institution." He would soon come to Bryn Mawr's remark, "I hate the place."

When the designs for Bryn Mawr were being developed, Woodrow was still Tommy, concerned with the numerous pleasures of his privileged existence as an undergraduate at the all-male College of New Jersey. He had been blissfully unaware of the work being done less than fifty miles away by a few prominent Philadelphia businessmen. These sensible men of affairs believed that a woman should be able to get a college degree. The founders of Bryn Mawr were well aware that over eighty American universities had already allowed women. (There were sixteen coeducational universities and colleges in Pennsylvania alone, including Swarthmore and Pennsylvania State College, later known as Penn State.) However, they were most impressed by the successful examples of all-women's schools to the north, such as Mount Holyoke, Smith, Vassar, Wellesley, and Wells College. They argued that the only thing missing from these schools' approach was a foundation in the Society of Friends' Quaker principles. Their goal was to create a female counterpart to the nearby Quaker liberal arts college, Haverford, which is all-male.

The occasion was Wilson's December 1884 job interview for a teaching position at Bryn Mawr. Thomas was busy interviewing people from Johns Hopkins and other places to fill the school's initial faculty positions. Herbert Adams and Richard Ely suggested him. Adams, who had previously assisted Wilson by acting as a reference for publishers, then personally encouraged his protégé to apply for a post at the young institution.

Given Wilson's archaic beliefs toward sex, interviewing with a woman would have been uncomfortable enough. It didn't help that Carry Thomas was barely his age (she was one week younger). He spent days before the interview tossing and turning in bed, terrified that he would never be able to take a position teaching women. He would "prefer to teach young men," he told Ellen. Indeed, he'd "rather teach men anywhere, and especially in the South, than girls at Bryn Mawr or anywhere else."

On the surface, the verbal sparring that undoubtedly began as soon as they sat down to dinner in Baltimore may have appeared to be the type of fun rivalry and struggle for control one might expect on a first date between two lively and intellectual young people who share many interests. Wilson must have foreseen this. He enjoyed the company of women and aimed to be chivalrous and funny. With his elegant black mustache, close-trimmed sideburns, and profusion of thick, perfectly barbered hair, the self-conscious young guy who professed to being "peculiarly susceptible" to "all feminine attractions" obviously believed that women would find him appealing. Dean Thomas might have drawn to him as much for her lively brown eyes, lovely voice, and attractive look as for her strong interest in academic pursuits, which she shared with Wilson.

Carey Thomas criticized Wilson as soon as they began their dinner, exuding an unmistakable air of superiority. He was taken aback. Rather than melting before him, she made him feel inadequate.

The bitter dose of reality was especially difficult to swallow because it was delivered by this domineering young woman. He was surely due respect from her because he was a man. However, Thomas believed his gender did not automatically entitle him to respect.

Knowing she had put him on the defensive, he was resolved to fight back, establishing himself as her peer and intellectual equal. If she was going to be dismissive and condescending, he would prove he was up to the task. He'd turn on the charm, soften her critical attitude, and win her over.

Over the many years that Woodrow Wilson had been intentionally ignoring the burgeoning movement in America for women's equal rights to school, work, and vote, Carey Thomas had completely embraced both the ideal of equality and the practical issues of achieving it. Despite being the same age, Thomas was significantly more accomplished. She had mastered numerous languages, earned multiple degrees, and outperformed him in a variety of other areas. Thomas was not only the driving force behind Bryn Mawr College, but also one of a small group of women who planned the foundation of Bryn Mawr School in Baltimore to prepare girls for college. It would open the following year, ensuring a consistent stream of applicants who could meet her stringent requirements.

She, like Wilson, was raised in a strongly religious family and, like him, carried racial and religious prejudices that married her progressive credentials. But, unlike him, she resisted norms that restricted women's participation in society. As a 14-year-old girl, she attended Anna Dickinson's evening lecture in Baltimore and immediately wrote her wholehearted affirmation of the speaker's message: women of intellect and talent, just like men, have a duty "to go out into the world" and elevate the human race. She was disgusted by the thought that God designed every woman to be a wife and mother, practically shrieking in her diary, "Bah!" Stuff and foolishness!" Even before college, she and her lover, Mamie Gwinn, were interested in atheism and free love. As a mature adult, she became more circumspect and restrained about religion and sex, yet she remained fiercely independent and iconoclastic. Most importantly, she was unwaveringly committed to women's social and political equality.

Wilson had every reason to warm Thomas, given the chance she was providing him. Over the next few months, it became evident that she was his only consistent supporter among Bryn Mawr's leadership. Her repeated suggestion helped keep his candidacy alive when the all-male board of trustees was hesitant to hire him. Furthermore, Wilson well understood the board's reluctance. Despite his high opinion of himself, he was aware that he lacked both teaching experience and a doctorate. Wilson worried in secret that he couldn't be a Bryn Mawr instructor since he couldn't read German at all."

When he finally received an offer for a teaching position, he should have understood that it was because of Thomas's conviction in him and her relentless lobbying for him. Instead, he whined about the terms. The offer was less than his desired amount. His title was insufficient. He wouldn't even be an "associate professor"—only an "associate," the lowest level on the faculty. His large ego was hurt. Rather than accept the sponsorship of the school's dean, who had helped him get the job, he would steadfastly refuse to express true gratitude for her patronage, simply because she was a woman.

She was a natural force that energized the institution and had an omnipresent influence on all aspects of campus life. For the next three years, whether Wilson liked it or not, Carey Thomas would be at the center of his professional life.

This did not prevent Wilson from defying her authority. In unsuccessful attempts to boost his reputation on the faculty, he went over Thomas' head to Rhoads several times. Ellen joined him in insulting the concept of a woman leading the school. "The Dean!""She sneered. "How ridiculous!"" To both of them, it was unnatural and improper for a woman to have an executive position, higher in the line of command than a male. Woodrow wrote to Ellen that women "do not have the same gifts as men." Their life must augment man's life.

Wilson consoled himself with the thought that as head of his history department, he would at least have some male autonomy. However, he was the lone faculty member in the department. Still, Carey Thomas constantly monitored him. Her perspective was that Wilson had the ability to decide what his courses would cover and how they would be taught, but only provided his actions were consistent with official Bryn Mawr policy. And as dean, she was responsible.

She worked tirelessly at her job and kept track of almost every faculty decision. She took complaints directly from students to control department heads. She selected Wilson's graduate fellows. When she had an idea, she acted on it immediately. Though he complained, Wilson was not even free to pick the time for his students' exams, as Dean Thomas's rules and standards applied to these minor details as well.

With such an enthusiastic and detail-oriented CEO as his boss, Wilson could have made it his mission to get along with her. Indeed, given their similar ages and scholarly interests, he might have suggested a partnership. The opportunity arrived when a book publisher offered that he and Thomas collaborate on a textbook. Wilson wrote to the publisher, without even telling her, saying he was very interested— but that he preferred to write the book himself.

While Carey Thomas had a friendly demeanor, it rapidly cooled when the subject shifted from work to casual talk. She was always eager to discuss school issues, but she had little interest in forming personal relationships with any of her faculty members. Her interactions with Wilson, like those with the rest of the academics and staff, were strictly professional. In summary, she possessed an executive temperament that Wilson would have admired in a male.

Wilson's patronizing attitude toward his female students was oppressive in the classroom. He purposely dominated class, drawing out all the oxygen, unable to consider what women may offer. "It was clear," a fellow pupil wrote, "that Mr. Wilson preferred to carry on the main discussion himself." However, he continued to worry about the students being "too docile." He also grumbled about the "strain" it put on him "to be all the year dominating"—blaming his own chauvinism on the quietly suffering Bryn Mawr scholars.

Wilson's intellectual snobbery towards women blinded him to their abilities. Cornell's president, with whom Salmon had studied at the University of Michigan and had read Wilson's book, cautioned her that she would be patronized despite her superior knowledge and credentials. "You must not anticipate," he said matter-of-factly. "Wilson will be able to help you a lot." He continued: "I shall be very much surprised if you find he knows nearly as much history as you do." He instructed her to remember that "it is better to give than to receive." According to Salmon, Wilson appeared to hardly acknowledge the presence of his female students. Wilson viewed her and the others "as an audience to whom he could express his views."

Her harsh assessment: "I am quite sure he never whole-heartedly believed in college education for women."

There was also evidence that Wilson's unease with the prospect of teaching women made the Bryn Mawr students uncomfortable with him. His first-year lectures on Greece and Rome drew seven pupils. In his advanced constitutional history course, he performed even worse. "I will have to let you into a deadly secret," he told a pal. "My entire class consists of one girl!"

Wilson attracted more students in the following years, and several of those who were satisfied with his being "unconscious of the presence of others, except as they served as an audience" considered his lectures polished and even inspiring. One woman described him as "the most interesting and inspiring college lecturer she'd ever heard." However, he became increasingly concerned with how to avoid teaching women. To him, the only positive thing about Bryn Mawr was the time it afforded for writing—so he spent as much time as possible composing political essays and a college textbook on government. Unfortunately, when he sent the writings to his Princeton friend Robert Bridges at Scribner's Magazine, they were all rejected, and the textbook proved difficult to complete despite the help of a graduate fellow.

Amazingly, Adams and Ely went with the plan. They disregarded the standard dissertation requirements and assured he would only have to take two written exams, which they would personally oversee to ensure he had "no chance" of failing. "We understand the case and you may rest assured it will be successfully tried," Adams promised him. Both would also finish Wilson's oral exam in under an hour. "You will pass that ordeal very easily," Adams emphasized.

Wilson's instructors gave him credit for his brief published work, Congressional Government, rather than a dissertation, although it was based on no fresh research and did not adhere to the school's rigorously empirical approach. On the day he finished his testing, Wilson enthusiastically informed his wife that his partners had given him "an exceedingly fair set of questions." They had made it simple, even though he "displayed considerable ignorance on some points."

That was all there was to it. The next day, he had his Ph.D. Wilson had only finished eighteen months of coursework at Johns Hopkins before dropping out. One year later, he just asked his mentors for a pass and received it. The contrast with the torture Carey Thomas had gone through to earn her doctorate couldn't have been greater. She completed three years of graduate coursework, taking hundreds of written exams along the way, and practically lived in libraries and archives conducting the meticulous original research required for her dissertation. Then, to demonstrate her understanding of the theory and grammar of Indo-Germanic linguistic evolution, she took four days of written exams and a three-hour oral test administered by the university's experts in nine disciplines. All these exams were conducted in German. Her degree required a unanimous faculty vote. There was no comparison to Wilson's "special consideration" for luck.

Wilson, armed with a gleaming new Ph.D., went to work looking for another position, bolstered by his wife's enthusiasm. Her sympathy for his plight as a teacher of women came from a distance, too, because despite their marriage and new home near school, husband and wife were once again relegated to letter buddies.

When Ellen was more than eight months pregnant, Wilson put her on a train to Georgia, believing it was best if she returned to her family to have the baby. It was a dangerous decision for a woman suffering from terrible morning sickness and other difficulties, especially since her own mother died of septicemia shortly after giving birth. For two nights, she rocked and banged through vast tracts of countryside, alone and cold, hoping that the train would not break down, as it so often did. When she landed in Georgia in the dark, it was only a matter of hours until she started having contractions that became more intense shortly after midnight. The baby arrived four and a half hours after daylight. Her delivery was "unquestionably hastened by the fatigues of the journey," as Wilson later admitted.

When the baby arrived, Ellen was struck with thoughts of her missing husband. She cried not "for the pain," but "for Woodrow." She selflessly advised him to "enjoy" himself because his "mind will now be less anxious." That is exactly what he had started doing even before hearing Ellen's news. After bidding her farewell at the station, he slipped away on a busman's holiday to Washington, where he "went around to see various officials," "watched the House and the Supreme Court," and took in "the excitements of going about and talking to all sorts of people, and seeing all sorts of things."

He undoubtedly loved not being woken up by the baby's two a.m. feedings, which allowed him to consistently get a decent night's sleep and dedicate his entire focus to his writing and job search. Even yet, finding another school to take him away from Bryn Mawr took far longer than he had hoped.

Wilson's displeasure at being surrounded by ladies who had abandoned their normal feminine roles grew. His performance demonstrated that. Students consistently said he was uninterested or unable to connect with them. He appeared to be more concerned with the quality of his own written lectures and oral delivery than with what was going on in the brains of his students. His lectures were clear and polished, but as one of his Bryn Mawr graduate colleagues noted, he appeared "more interested in [the] manner of expression than he was in the thoughts and ideals expressed."

Many of these lectures expanded on Wilson's well-known criticism of Congress's do-nothing committee structure. However, not long after he graduated from Johns Hopkins, one tenacious committee in Congress demonstrated once more how it might bring an issue to the entire Senate. In January 1887, the Select Committee on Woman Suffrage achieved the first-ever floor vote for Aaron Sargent's women's suffrage amendment. It was a topic Bryn Mawr's government students would have loved. There is no evidence that Wilson ever brought it up, although the national press gave it plenty of coverage.

While opposing the women's suffrage amendment (as it would till the end), the New York Times was impressed by the number of votes it obtained on its first effort. Counting the absent senators who committed their support, it "received the support of over thirty-six percent of the Senators," which the Times recognized was "not a desperate showing by any means." "If votes are to be weighed as well as counted," the editors said, noting that several of the most prominent men in the Senate had voted aye. "The ladies may congratulate themselves on the names on their side." The Philadelphia Inquirer, to which Wilson in Bryn Mawr had easy access, published extracts from the discussion, with the title criticizing the majority of "ungallant men" who voted nay.

The Senate's extended time for legislation showed it was taken seriously. Republican senator Joseph Dolph of Oregon, one of several who testified in support of the amendment during the daylong debate, stated that "history is full of the records of great deeds by women"—a statement that Wilson's Bryn Mawr classmates would have agreed with. "They have ruled kingdoms," Dolph reminded his colleagues, "and commanded armies. They have excelled in statecraft, shone in literature, and, rising above their surroundings and breaking free from the constraints of custom and tyranny, they have stood alongside men in the arts and sciences."

Dixon suggested Wilson for an honorary degree from Wake Forest in June 1887, confident that it would boost his friend's résumé and possibilities for a new job. But making the pitch was no easy task. In the face of skepticism from Wake Forest faculty and trustees, Dixon resorted to seriously inflating Wilson's experience, claiming he had "graduated in law from the University of Virginia," was a "very able lawyer," and had been "the most distinguished student who ever got his degree at Johns Hopkins"—despite the fact that Wilson had dropped out of law school, never had a paying law client other than his mother, and received no honors or distinctions at Johns Hopkins. As trustees continued to ask questions, Dixon "waxed eloquent" with more hyperbole, convincing them to choose Wilson for the honor.

He was always referred to as "Dr. Wilson" in Presbyterian church records and government documents, and many of Woodrow Wilson's biographers utilized the title for his father. However, Joseph Wilson never received a doctorate in divinity, or any other postgraduate degree. When he was a young pastor, he got an honorary degree from a small Presbyterian college in central Georgia, which gave him the right to call himself "Dr."

Six weeks later, on April 15, Wilson got a telegram from his younger brother saying their mother had died. Janet Woodrow Wilson died on a Sunday afternoon, alone except for "only the servant with her." Wilson would be late to the funeral. "My heart is almost broken," he confessed to Ellen.

Part II: Governor and President

Chapter 5: 'Shall I Not Accept?'

WILSON'S STEAMER ARRIVED AT THE pier in Hamilton Harbour early on a Monday morning, delivering on the Thomas Cook travel agency's advertised promise of "forty hours from frost to flowers." Balmy Bermuda in mid-January was a nice respite from the severe weather he had left behind. Only a few weeks previously, he had delivered his annual report for 1906 to the Princeton board of trustees, daydreaming about escaping from his typical household and academic routines to this island vacation.

As he walked down Front Street to his hotel, Wilson's daydreams included more than pink sand beaches, rocky coves, and color-drenched blossoms. In the days leading up to his departure from Princeton, the publisher of his History of the American People managed to push Wilson to the brink of becoming the Democratic nominee for U.S. Senate from New Jersey. Colonel George Harvey, president of Harper & Brothers, relied on the state party's most prominent figure, James "Sugar Jim" Smith Jr. of Essex County, to coordinate all of the votes his machine controlled. Once again, the undergraduate fantasies of "Thomas W. Wilson, Senator from Virginia," and later "T. Woodrow Wilson, Senator from Georgia," came to the forefront. Now, however, the middle-aged man's political ambitions have surpassed the boy's. He envisioned himself president, not senator.

With the 17th Amendment six years away, state legislatures continued to select U.S. senators, with Republicans controlling New Jersey's. As a result, the Democratic nomination served no electoral purpose. While some in politics may consider it an honor, Wilson's acceptance of the nomination is more likely to brand him as someone hungry for office than to increase his appeal as a serious candidate. The only thing it guaranteed was a loss in his first effort, and a slew of questions in the Princeton boardroom about the depth of his dedication to the university. For these reasons, Wilson declined the offer six days before boarding the SS Bermudian.

She invited him to supper at her house the following evening, which happened to be his final night on the island. Before leaving Bermuda the next day, he left her a message openly characterizing her as a woman "whom I can so entirely admire and enjoy." He sent her gifts, wrote her more loving letters, and planned to return to Bermuda alone as soon as possible, which happened to be the following January.

During the five weeks they spent together in early 1908, Wilson poured his heart out to her. They saw each other every day. While he lazed away the afternoons in her hammock, she and her mother brought him tea and "coddled him." They loved conversing about "foolish things" during lengthy walks on the beach, oblivious to the rumors that circulated around the island's limited social circle. More importantly, Peck listened sympathetically to his opinions on life, literature, and politics. Almost immediately, she recalled, theirs was a "perfect comradeship." He accompanied her to tea dances and dinners. As they lay on the beach, he read her poetry from The Oxford Book of English Verse.

It only heightened his interest in Peck, who readily supported all his political ideas. Nonetheless, she had an independent streak. When Sarah and Wilson talked about marriage, she accused him of wanting "a doormat wife." Wilson didn't refute it. "I am sure," he said; "if you were my wife you would be very pleased to do anything I should wish." That was almost true while they were in their greatest infatuation. Peck willingly accommodated Wilson's "dictatorial tone" toward her sex, which was displayed even in public when he gave a speech in Hamilton denouncing women's suffrage.

Bryan was consumed by fire a third time in the fall of 1908. Wilson disclosed to Peck that he was seriously considering running for president in four years. With false modesty, he claimed he did not seek the presidency, saying that no man of principle would "risk the appearance of personal ambition." Nonetheless, he persisted in seeking her approval for his objectives, admitting that he had been "born political" and was yearning to leave Princeton and enter the political arena.

Whereas Ellen's unwavering support for her husband was tempered by concerns about what a run for office would do to his delicate health, Peck wholeheartedly supported his aspirations. Wilson's other wife offered him the unquestioning validation he wanted.

Their primarily long-distance relationship, interspersed by Peck's occasional travels to the mainland, grew stronger in the spring of 1909, when she informed Wilson that she intended to return from Bermuda to file for divorce. The same Woodrow Wilson who had openly condemned the state's permissive divorce rules was thrilled with the news. He gushed to Peck that her impending divorce and transfer to New York would boost his chances of being with her "a hundredfold!"

Throughout his latter years as Princeton president, Wilson turned to Mary Peck for support in his increasingly heated battles with the university's board of trustees. Long knives were drawn for him. "Discord begets hate," a contemporary biographer observed. By 1909, the boardroom was "sizzling with malice." Wilson himself felt "broken, battered, and weary." Peck continually urged his leave from the institution to run for parliament. In turn, he gave her moral support for her decision to divorce Thomas Peck.

During these rising tensions with the Princeton trustees, more than simply Wilson's position was eroding. Even as he engaged his opponents on the faculty and board in an attempt to maintain his authority as president of the university, he considered abandoning academia entirely. His tempting plan B was to pursue a career in elective politics, which had been his lifetime desire.

In January 1910, three months after his boardroom humiliation, Wilson's political ambitions became more realistic. His eager publicist George Harvey once again contacted "Sugar Jim" Smith, this time to urge the New Jersey boss's support for Wilson's election as governor. The man dubbed by a Tammany Hall stalwart as "the greatest one-man politician in the country," and father of three Princeton kids, agreed to Harvey's proposal. They would first appoint him governor, and then use that as a springboard to compete for president in 1912.

Following this promising development, Wilson's natural intransigence in dealing with his Princeton opponents escalated into downright violence. He purposefully carried the campus controversy beyond the boardroom, framing the debate over the site of the graduate school as a battle for "democracy." He persuaded a friendly writer at the New York Times to chastise Princeton's prospective graduate school benefactor for supporting "certain ideals"—the separation of undergraduate and graduate students—that Wilson felt "wholly unsuitable and indeed likely to be distinctly demoralizing."He left Princeton right away for a three-week solo vacation to Bermuda, feeling "wounded." He was devastated that she couldn't accompany him and made plans to see her just before leaving New York. He began writing to her right away from aboard and continued to do so once he landed.

On Valentine's Day, he wrote to Mary Peck and Ellen, telling them how much he missed them. "I adore you and long for you, my sweetheart. "You mean everything to me," he assured Ellen in a two-paragraph note. In a lengthy letter to his "sweet, incomparable" Mary, he admitted that the island was "too desperately lonely for words!" because she was not present. He bemoaned that going to the place where they shared so many memories just made him "more lonely!" Peck also seemed to find separation difficult. "Ah! "If only I were there," she lamented, urging her "best beloved" to return soon. While Peck was still in Bermuda, Ellen and her daughter Nell paid a surprise visit to his New York residence. Ellen wrote to her husband that they had "a delightful little visit," without revealing what was discussed.

Wilson's increasingly public conflict with the Princeton board was creating waves of national attention, aided by publisher Harvey's tireless advertising efforts. The coverage in the South was particularly complimentary, with almost all of it citing Wilson as a prospective presidential candidate. A glowing Associated Press story that went coast-to-coast openly endorsed the notion, praising Princeton's president for having "the courage of his convictions."

Wilson's media campaign to tie the "cruel hands" of the Princeton trustees ended abruptly on May 22, 1910. Only the day before, he made national headlines for his speech criticizing "evil corporations," a political theme that relied on his record of standing up to Princeton's plutocrat alumni and benefactors. But on Sunday morning, the top page of the New York Times revealed Dean West's ultimate win. "Gift of $10,000,000 Left to Princeton," the headline read, above a piece noting that, unlike the previous vow Wilson had successfully scotched, this donation was irrevocable. The donor died three days prior, and his will named Dean West co-executor of the estate, with "almost absolute power" over its disposition.

The Princeton board was unwilling to reject this donation. They overwhelmingly voted for Dean West's proposal to develop the graduate school campus at the place Wilson had so forcefully rejected. Wilson finally gave up after running out of options. "I deemed it necessary in the circumstances," he wrote a pal on May 30, "that I should accept defeat." He would "no longer fight" over the graduate school site. His relationship with the board, he admitted, appeared "now rather hopeless."

He just wanted to go away. He fled immediately, a defeated man in a circumstance he admitted to his daughter Jessie was "most humiliating," for what would be his final summer vacation as a teacher. Only months later, he would publicly resign as Princeton's head.

Wilson hadn't met either man. But Smith had already agreed to Harvey's proposal to name him governor, and Watterson had been endorsing Wilson for president in his newspaper and syndicated column for months. Watterson, now seventy years old, began his career in the Confederate army as a military aide to Nathan Bedford Forrest, the man responsible for the worst war crime committed during the Civil War—the massacre of hundreds of surrendering Union soldiers, most of whom were Black, at Fort Pillow, Tennessee—and who later became the first Grand Wizard of the Ku Klux Klan. Watterson and Smith had both served in Congress and had spent many years working on campaigns. Both veteran politicians were eager to meet with their chosen candidate in person and learn that he was fully committed to taking the plunge.

Their dinner gathering turned into a conference, which lasted until midnight. Wilson had completed his mental transition from intellectual to politician when they adjourned. The following day, he wrote to a friend that "the question of my nomination for governor is the mere preliminary of a plan to nominate me for president in 1912." It was perfect timing, coming just as his Princeton opponents were agreeing that "restoration of proper feeling [among the] Board, Faculty, and Alumni cannot begin while Woodrow remains."

He immediately began contacting his closest allies in the board disputes of recent years. He prudently sought their counsel on whether he should run, rather than revealing that he had already made up his mind. He secured their support on almost every occasion. It was a good start for his campaign because most of them were extremely wealthy.

On September 15, Wilson entered his new career with confidence. He was now the Democratic candidate for Governor of New Jersey. His selection at the convention was a triumph for the state's Democratic Party leaders, especially Sugar Jim and his son-in-law, James Nugent, chairman of the New Jersey Democratic State Committee. Together, they organized the nomination of a man the delegates had never met and knew little about. To the day of his nomination, Wilson followed Harvey's suggestion to "duck" the concerns, declining any press inquiries on the grounds that "discussing important issues" would be inappropriate because he was not "a candidate seeking the nomination." In the end, none of this mattered; the ruling camarilla had made its decision.

He became the Democratic nominee with less than two months till Election Day. For the brief campaign that followed, Wilson relied primarily on his promoters' counsel, particularly George Harvey, who devised a cautious strategy for the inexperienced candidate. Instead of the customary heavy schedule of small meetings across the state where voters may directly connect with the nominee, they would focus on a small number of huge audiences. Instead of a "whirlwind," each county in the state would be assigned a single formal address. The Democratic Party chairman explained that this was done to "save the strength" of the candidate. The tiny size of New Jersey, the fourth-smallest state in the US, would make the schedule manageable.

Wilson's Republican opponent was Vivian M. Lewis, a former journalist, National Guard captain, and government lawyer who had previously served as the General Assembly's majority leader and was now the Commissioner of Banking and Insurance. In his acceptance speech, Lewis supported progressive initiatives such as direct primary elections for the state's governor and members of Congress, and a public utilities commission with rate-making authority. However, New Jersey's Republican platform ignored these reforms while praising President Taft for his pro-business policies. Lewis voluntarily linked his candidacy to the Taft administration's accomplishments, exposing him to attacks on Republicans in Washington for their recent tax increases in the form of the widely unpopular Payne-Aldrich Tariff

Act.

Wilson saw this opportunity to criticize Republican tariff policies as a gift. As a southerner, he was raised in an anti-tariff heritage. The cotton economy in the South benefited nothing from protectionist trade barriers, therefore the tariff was always its greatest enemy. Wilson, as a college student, had chosen to debate the protective tariff. His first overt political act, as a young lawyer in Georgia, was to testify against agricultural tariffs in a field hearing of the US Tariff Commission. For years, he had written and spoken out against protective tariffs.

Unfortunately for Republican candidates, the nation's 2,600 daily and weekly newspapers were among the hardest hurt by the new tariffs. They were now facing sky-high newsprint prices after Taft used his authority under the new law to levy a 25% retaliatory tariff on lower-cost Canadian newsprint. Unsurprisingly, thousands of editors and publishers responded by launching fierce attacks on the Taft administration and Republicans everywhere.

Wilson won the election thanks to a national Democratic surge. His 54% vote share was mirrored by statewide support for Democratic legislative candidates, increasing the party's majority in the General Assembly while leaving Republicans with a 57% advantage in the Senate. Democrats added six new governors and fifty-five seats in the House, including four from New Jersey. This was the final time that U.S. senators were chosen by state legislatures, and the Democrats took full advantage: the party's wins in state legislative races resulted in nine more Democratic seats in the United States Senate.

Ten days before Christmas, men and women from the Southern Society staged a holiday luncheon for New Jersey's governor-elect at the Waldorf Astoria in New York, to the tune of "Dixie" and rebel screams. The toastmaster was Tennessee transplant William G. McAdoo, president of New York's Hudson and Manhattan Railroad, who introduced Wilson as the country's "future president." The cover of the evening's program featured "the old negro mammy," which the New York Tribune delicately interpreted as a tribute to "the old Southern life."

Although he would not be sworn in as governor for over two months, the Atlanta Journal was already imagining McAdoo's place in a

Wilson presidential administration. "The South is certainly entitled," the paper opined, "to the party's next presidential nominee"—and Wilson would be "eminently acceptable." Finally, the editors announced, the South will "be given its due."

Between the election and his inauguration, he wrote to her frequently, complimenting her on her "beauty," "extraordinary vivacious charm," and "power of love." He cooed over her "wonderful combination of qualities and charms," calling her "adorable!" He wished to see her. "I miss you dreadfully," he admitted, somewhat pathetically. "I am desperately lonely—as lonely as I was when I walked away from Pier 47 the day you sailed."

Peck missed him just as much. "Do you know the Oceana leaves New York on Saturdays, making a quick trip down here, stopping for a few hours, and returning directly to New York?" demanded the captain. "Can't you come?"

He couldn't. Bemoaning the loss of the luxurious luxury he had enjoyed at Princeton, he criticized the rigorous rules of his chosen new life. "There is nothing in it for individual gain! Every individual comfort and delight (for example, and most importantly, the freedom to travel to Bermuda) has been eliminated," he complained. "I am in revolt, and wish I were—in Bermuda."

Chapter 6: 'The Least Part of It'

Wilson has been campaigning nationally since the day he was elected governor. It was a tremendous aspiration for a new politician, but not unrealistic. His powerful relationships in journalism from his years of writing and publishing, together with his several friends among wealthy Princeton graduates from his years of fundraising, had already established the foundation of a viable campaign.

George Harvey's highly effective advertising and publicity campaign on Wilson's behalf, which leveraged his influence at Harper's Weekly, Metropolitan Magazine, the North American Review, and the Harper & Brothers publishing house, resulted in positive coverage of Wilson in newspapers and magazines across the country. Harvey began promoting Wilson for president four years before he was nominated for governor. Throughout Wilson's first year in office, Harvey commissioned and wrote pieces promoting Wilson for president, both for his own magazines and others.

In the Northeast, Wilson's extensively publicized campaign against Princeton trustees, followed by his attention-grabbing attack against bossism in New Jersey that continued after the election, drew many powerful allies from outside the Garden State. One of them, Dudley Field Malone, was a well-known public speaker who worked as assistant corporation attorney for the City of New York and had established a solid reputation as a surrogate for William Jennings Bryan during the previous presidential campaign. As the son-in-law of New York's Democratic U.S. Senator James O'Gorman, he had political clout that far exceeded his twenty-seven years. So did his natural abilities as a lawyer and campaigner.

By March, Wilson had a de facto presidential campaign team. His campaign manager was William F. McCombs, the Arkansas-born son of a Confederate cavalry veteran and Wilson's former Princeton pupil, who had since graduated from Harvard Law School and practiced law in New York City. Frank P. Stockbridge, the campaign's press agent, was a journeyman reporter and editorial writer with two decades of experience writing for various New York newspapers. However, Wilson refused to disclose having a "campaign manager" or a "press agent," meticulously maintaining the deception that he was not a contender.

Stockbridge learned a lot about Wilson's points of view during their extensive private conversation time on this trip. In preparation for their journey to Denver, where women already had the vote and Wilson would attend a dinner reception organized by Bryn Mawr graduates, he told his press director that he was "definitely and irreconcilably opposed to woman suffrage," and that a "woman's place was in the home." Women's participation in "public activities of a political nature," he warned Stockbridge, was "degrading to the sex."

But it was more than his opposition to women voting and working outside the home. Wilson despised female suffragists, whom he described to Stockbridge as "unsexed" and "masculinized." Drawing on his personal experiences with Carey Thomas and others at Bryn Mawr, he expressed his distaste with "the type of woman who took an active part in the suffrage agitation." These "ladies," the governor complained, were "totally abhorrent" to him. Stockbridge, a New Englander from Maine and Massachusetts whose personal views on race and gender were far more liberal than Wilson's, naturally kept the governor's most insulting remarks hidden.

By this moment, the California women's suffrage campaign had been nearly a generation in the making. A women's suffrage amendment was on the ballot fifteen years ago and lost by ten percentage points, 55-45. The proposition had been backed in Southern California, where Wilson was currently speaking, but it was heavily rejected by San Francisco voters. Partisan divisions exacerbated the situation. In the previous campaign, Republican senator Aaron Sargent's widow, Ellen Sargent, and her daughter, ophthalmologist Elizabeth C. Sargent, transformed their home into a statewide campaign headquarters and donated significantly to the effort. For eight months, the Sargent mansion acted as a hotel for visiting suffrage lecturers such as Susan B. Anthony and Anna Howard Shaw. Fifteen years later, the entire Republican leadership in California supported women's suffrage, with Hiram Johnson, the state's progressive Republican governor, leading the way. A Republican state senator authored the law that placed the suffrage proposal on the ballot, which was adopted by a Republican state legislature.

However, prominent Democratic Party officials remained against the proposed state constitutional amendment. John Bunyan Sanford, chairman of the California Democratic Party Caucus, wrote the official ballot argument opposing Proposition 4. "The mother's influence is important at home. "She can do little good by gadding the streets and ignoring her children," Sanford stated. Even in the Los Angeles Times, he was less conciliatory. "Woman Suffrage is a disease," he argued, "a political hysteria" that will lead to "crime, divorce, and 'fallen women.'" The progressive Democrat maintained, "Woman suffrage is not progressive." "It is a step backward in civilizational progress."

Wilson, aware of these issues, avoided discussing suffrage in his speech in Los Angeles. Instead, he offered a more abstract argument that avoided immediately hurting initiative supporters while emphasizing his philosophical similarities to suffrage opponents. Six months before California voters went to the polls, he urged Democratic supporters to disregard Jefferson's impassioned introduction to the Declaration.The experienced academic and political scientist recognized that he was making a familiar point. The trivialization of Jefferson's opening lines in the Declaration had long been a mainstay of southern Democratic justifications for denying Black people the right to vote. The idea that a portion of the Declaration of Independence was not the original Declaration has been claimed for almost as long in justification of laws excluding women from voting.

However, rejection of this argument had an equally lengthy history. In the 1850s, abolitionists who also supported women's voting rights mocked the notion that the phrase "all men are created equal" did not represent the human race. On the eve of the Civil War, Wendell Phillips, who had stood firm with Elizabeth Cady Stanton and Lucretia Mott at the World Anti-Slavery Society Convention in London in 1840, declared it "gross dishonesty or ignorance" to claim that "life, liberty, and the pursuit of happiness" are not the unalienable rights of men and women alike. Twentieth-century Democrats did not necessarily appreciate Wilson's interpretation of Jefferson's meaning.

Democratic Representative Edward Taylor of Colorado, speaking in Congress less than a year after Wilson's speech in Los Angeles, denounced it explicitly. "Let us show to the world that we believe in the Declaration of Independence," he exclaimed. The notion that men and women do not have equal unalienable rights is only for "the partisan, prejudiced, biased, and smaller minds that have always desperately opposed any advance of womanhood," he stated. He labeled the argument a "disgrace."

Despite the intense marketing, voters turned out on November 7 to vote against the new governor and the Democratic legislature. In a stunning shift from the Democratic sweep that had just propelled Wilson to power, the election gave Republicans control of both houses of the state legislature. The outcome gained national attention, prompting two Democratic presidential candidates, Ohio governor Judson Harmon and Speaker of the House Champ Clark, to declare that Wilson had been rejected by his own state.

This unpleasant news was quickly followed by two major campaign disasters.

In January 1912, the New York Sun released a letter Wilson sent four years previously criticizing William Jennings Bryan. In this letter, Wilson supported a fellow Princeton trustee's critique of Bryan's "socialistic, populistic, anti-property crusade," and expressed a desire to "knock Mr. Bryan once for all into a cocked hat!" The timing couldn't have been worse. Wilson was courting Bryan's progressive followers at the time the letter was published in the newspapers. His relationship with Bryan had begun months before, when Ellen went to considerable lengths to organize an introductory meal for the two men, which went well. He and Bryan were scheduled to appear together at a huge Democratic fundraiser in a few days.

Wilson promptly huddled with his main aides, McCombs and Malone. McCombs proposed blaming the letter's publishing on "Wall Street." However, complaining about the leak would not be sufficient. Bryan's main concern was hearing Wilson's explanation and determining whether he still maintained the same opinion.

By chance, Wilson supporter Josephus Daniels, the editor of the

Raleigh News and Observer with whom Wilson first became acquainted in 1909 (and whom he had recently visited during a trip to North Carolina), was accompanying Bryan to Washington for the Democratic fundraiser at which Bryan and Wilson would be featured speakers. Daniels did his best to calm Bryan's agitated nerves on the way. When they arrived in Washington, Malone and his father-in-law, New York Senator James O'Gorman, took over the case.

On December 7, 1911, in a private room at New York's Manhattan Club, Wilson told his most loyal advocate that Harper's Weekly's support was harming his standing among anti-Wall Street Democrats, particularly in the West. Many of them assumed, however incorrectly, that the magazine's editor was close with "the interests."

Wilson couldn't afford such affiliations. He was already having trouble fending off accusations of antipathy toward organized labor based on his public utterances while Princeton's president. Only two years ago, in his baccalaureate address, he lambasted unions for their "economically disastrous" work restrictions. "Labor is standardized by the trades unions," he claimed, so that the employee can "give as little as he may for his wages," and "no one may volunteer anything beyond the minimum." He now needed to get away from those pronouncements.

In these challenging conditions, Wilson felt that Harper's Weekly, which was supposed to have ties to Wall Street, presented an appearance problem that could only be resolved by discontinuing the magazine's support for his candidacy. Harvey consented to his request, and the evening ended on an unpleasant tone.

However, the gloomy insinuations that Harper's Weekly and its editor lacked independence from Wall Street were based on questionable evidence. Harvey was a professional journalist. In 1893, he retired as managing editor of Joseph Pulitzer's New York World to pursue his desire of independence from paymasters. He wanted to own and operate his own publication. He earned the money by working as an entrepreneur for five years, establishing streetcar lines. They were developed using construction loans from New York businessmen such as J.P. Morgan and Thomas Fortune Ryan.

With the proceeds from this venture, he was able to withdraw from business entirely and return to full-time journalism as his own master, purchasing the North American Review in 1899 and becoming its editor in chief. Later that year, Harper & Brothers' family owners approached him to become president of the publishing house and editor of Harper's Weekly, citing his journalism and business experience as qualifications. At the time, the publishing house was experiencing financial difficulties and required a turnaround.

After that, Harvey remained silent. But Wilson's public denials of what he said at the dinner shattered Watterson's perception of the man. The North Carolinian attempted to correct the record and more. He called Wilson a liar, provided additional facts about their dinner chat, and demanded that independent arbiters be established to determine who was telling the truth. In retrospect, Wilson historian Arthur Link described the affair as such a shock to Wilson's presidential campaign that it "threatened to wreck it altogether."

It appeared no less frightening to commentators at the time. James C. Hemphill, editor of the Richmond Times-Dispatch who had previously editorialized in support of Wilson, described it as "the most remarkable story of political ingratitude and personal infidelity I have ever known." It involved, according to him, "cold blooded selfishness and utter disregard of all political common sense." The spectacular row erupted on top pages across the country.

Wilson quickly altered strategy after understanding that McCombs' attempt to reject the news and his own straightforward denial had been ineffective. Instead of avoiding and rejecting, he chose to embrace the important truths and wear Watterson's and others' criticism as a badge of honor. He would go on the offensive against "the interests." This would entail directly criticizing his old pals, but he intended to remain above the conflict. To convey the tough message, he went to Dudley Field Malone.

The prediction for Detroit on January 18, 1912, was "snow and colder." The weather closely mirrored the headline in that morning's Detroit Free Press declaring Watterson "Shocked by Governor's Cold Avowal He Thought Col. Harvey's Support Was Injurious." The snow and ice matched the cold shoulder Wilson and his proxy were going to give Harper's Weekly, Harvey, and Watterson.

Prior to this midnight occurrence, Wilson was "besieged all afternoon and evening by newspapers who begged him to make some sort of answer." However, the governor would only state that Watterson was a "nice old gentleman." He left it to Malone to put the already strained ties into deep freeze. Until now, Malone and Wilson had been traveling together on their Michigan campaign swing. However, Wilson planned his entrance for the large gathering in Detroit so Malone could precede him onstage. This allowed Malone to speak about the scandal without Wilson present.

The experienced attorney wasted no time in filing his allegations. Before the public opinion jury, which was represented in person by the rally's over two thousand attendees, he referred to Harvey and Watterson as "the enemies of the people," rather than by name. Furthermore, "newspapers of the last few weeks show whom the enemies of the people consider dangerous," according to Malone. Indeed, "enemies... who would besmirch a character so above question as that of Governor Wilson," claimed he, "do not bother to shoot unless they see it is worthwhile." They deserved "ignominy and contempt." But Wilson promised to punish them merely with "silence." Of course, Wilson was given this privilege because Malone was fighting for him.

For Wilson, forsaking well-meaning friends was an expensive way to handle the situation. The story eventually went down, but not before additional press inquiries drew unwanted attention to the campaign. Two weeks after the New York World editorial, the New York Times was still raising difficult questions. Weighing all of the remarks and correspondence that had finally been made public, the publication concluded that the episode demonstrated a severe fault in Wilson's character that may disqualify him. "The question," according to the newspaper, is "whether Woodrow Wilson, with these infirmities of temperament, does not lack some of the highly essential qualifications always associated with the great office to which he aspires."

On January 31, the front page of the Baltimore Sun ran seven separate items about the issue over Wilson's "veracity." Coincidentally, these pieces appeared on page one alongside a favorable report on

Maryland's women's suffrage campaign. Max Eastman, a recent Ph.D. student of Wilson's Johns Hopkins classmate John Dewey, had delivered the keynote lecture the night before in support of the "Maryland Statewide Unlimited Woman Suffrage" bill, which was then pending in the Annapolis legislature.

That same year, Wilson openly stated why he believed women should not vote. "Women," he told the Bermuda Royal Gazette, "do not really want the franchise." It would be worse if they did, because, unlike men, they ignore a candidate's "ability" and are "not a little influenced by charm of manners." Privately, Wilson was more fanatical. "My chief argument," he stated to a British acquaintance, is that "the family and the present division of duties between husband and wife" would "be absolutely altered" if women were granted the ability to vote.

Woodrow Wilson's extraordinarily brief gubernatorial administration in Trenton, New Jersey, which began in January 1911 and ended two years later, is sometimes labeled as "progressive," and in many ways it was. During his two years in government, he signed four important measures addressing electoral reform, corrupt practices, utility regulation, and workers' compensation. Wilson, however, refused to participate in voting for women.

Thomas Dixon's bestselling racist and sexist tales of a romantic Ku Klux Klan sparked a national outcry, but no literary franchise in the early twentieth century was more lucrative than L. Frank Baum's Oz series. Baum had already published six national bestsellers by the time Wilson took the governor's oath, dreams of a female utopia in which all rightful rulers are women.

Baum, a Republican newspaper editor who had long editorialized in support of women's suffrage, was influenced by his wife, a feminist whom he met while she was a student at Cornell, and her mother, Matilda Joslyn Gage—one of the original NAWSA leaders, along with Susan B. Anthony and Elizabeth Cady Stanton. Baum originally envisaged the realm of Oz at the Gages' upstate New York home, where the three suffragist icons were editing the first three volumes of their History of Woman Suffrage. His mother-in-law's guidance influenced large portions of his novels. Baum, like Dixon, created his own theatrical extravaganza, The Wizard of Oz, which was the most successful stage musical of the time. Featuring prominent female characters, it toured the country with two companies for eight years.

This steady flow of propaganda for women's political equality helped the campaign for women's voting rights make extraordinary headway in state legislatures across the country. While other governors advocated for women's suffrage, Wilson could take comfort in the fact that no president or major party presidential candidate had yet embraced the federal amendment. Grover Cleveland, who served with Wilson on the Princeton board of trustees, continued to push against women's suffrage even after leaving government. "Sensible and responsible women do not want to vote," Cleveland told the Ladies' Home Journal. McKinley supported women's suffrage, but he never campaigned for it or proclaimed support for the federal amendment. Roosevelt, who could have been expected to do so at some point during his seven years in the White House given his state-level support for the cause, instead chose to build on McKinley's record of appointing women to federal positions.

Taft continued to encourage suffragists after assuming the presidency. During his first year in office, he gave an address recognizing women's contributions as critical to "the future of modern civilization and the growth of popular self-government." In a call to action, he contrasted women's enormous contributions with their political helplessness. "Women are today and always have been," he added, "the leaders in all great moral reforms; yet as a disfranchised class they are powerless to aid in bringing about any reforms that depend upon legislative or governmental action." Taft closed his remarks by supporting the global struggle for women's suffrage. "Now that there is a world-wide movement among women to demand the political power to do their part in the world's work, they have a right," he stated, to offer "support and help in working for this greatest of all reforms."

On April 14, 1910, three months into Wilson's governorship, Taft became the first president to speak at a NAWSA convention. The lines to enter the sumptuous Arlington Hotel in Washington, D.C., stretched down the street. The president was greeted with a standing ovation as hundreds of white-robed delegates waved their handkerchiefs. But, rather than supporting the federal amendment, Taft said that his attitude had just shifted. While he had previously been a "orthodox" suffragist, he now admits, "I have modified my views somewhat."

With women taking on responsibilities in nearly every field and popular culture now awash in books, plays, music, and art extolling the virtues of expanding the franchise, it would be up to a future president to provide the movement for women's voting rights with a full-throated champion in the White House. As the fight for the Democratic candidacy narrowed in the summer of 1912, Wilson was resolved not to be that candidate.

Chapter 7: The Suffrage Inaugural

The Chicago Coliseum reopened its doors for its second national political convention in six weeks on August 5. Teddy Roosevelt's newly formed National Progressive Party was already generally known as the Bull Moose Party, following the candidate's repeated statement during the Republican convention: "I feel like a bull moose!" From the moment the twenty-sixth president mounted the stage until Election Day, the presidential campaign was rife with battle cries from pro- and anti-women's suffrage activists.

When Jane Addams seconded his nomination, she emphasized Roosevelt's support for women's suffrage. Before addressing the stage, she received a telegram from the former president requesting that she explain his dedication to women's voting rights "without qualification or equivocation."" Make it "as strong as you can," he instructed, and she did exactly that. Roosevelt was so impressed by Addams' words that, after the convention, he requested that her address be published as a pamphlet and disseminated around the country.

The overwhelming support from Addams nearly did not materialize. In addition to being one of the country's best-known suffragists, she was an ardent supporter for equal rights and served on the NAACP board. She became sharply disillusioned when, at the opening of the Bull Moose convention, Roosevelt announced that, while his new party would seat Black delegates from northern states, in the South he would rely on "the best white men," trusting in them "to create a situation by which the colored men of the South will ultimately get justice." The candidate's statements were reminiscent of Woodrow Wilson, who, as an academic, had regularly referred to the "better whites" as particularly qualified to reign in the southern states.

Addams struggled to reconcile her admiration for Roosevelt's pro-suffrage stance with his denial of "the rights of the negroes," but she tried. In the pages of the NAACP magazine The Crisis, she explained her decision, pointing out that the Republican and Bull Moose conventions both had Black delegates, although the Democratic National Convention did not. Furthermore, in the South, even "under so-called Republican protection," only white Democrats were eligible to vote. Roosevelt was questioning "the traditional shibboleths of both parties," she stated. In theory, Roosevelt's progressive white Southern men would battle the Democrats for Black people's rights more effectively than the Republicans.

It was a lame apology. Roosevelt's blatant attempt to curry favor with extremely prejudiced white southern Democrats lacked not only morality, but also common sense. As the Philadelphia Inquirer pointed out, it was doomed to fail because southern Democrats could choose their own candidate. "The South will stand solidly by Wilson," the publication rightly predicted. Perhaps realizing this fact, Addams chose to support the party and the candidate holding the suffrage banner.

Wilson's friend Oswald Garrison Villard, the editor of the New York Evening Post, was another person who attempted to persuade Wilson to commit. A month after the Baltimore convention, on August 13, Villard traveled to Trenton for a three-hour meeting with the Democratic nominee, pressing him on women's suffrage. However, the candidate persevered in his attempt to skirt the issue of state rights. "I labored with him," the disheartened editor confessed to a suffrage advocate in Boston who inquired about Wilson's position, but to "no avail." Villard concluded that Wilson "would prefer defeat" to backing the suffrage amendment, "in which he does not believe."

As the campaign progressed, Wilson closed his eyes and ears to the growing call for women's political equality. In a September speech at Tremont Temple in Boston, Wilson said the only women's right he recognized was "the right of women to bear children." In Denver, he urged industry to be "regardful of the weakness of women."

With only a few weeks until Election Day, the Wilson campaign made a final swing through New York, Roosevelt's stronghold and the greatest source of electoral votes in America. His campaign had gathered a friendly Democratic Party throng at the spectacular new Beaux-Arts opera house at the Brooklyn Academy of Music. Wilson was performing in a packed venue, with both balconies overflowing, and everything was going according to plan.

Wilson, along with many suffrage activists, did not completely understand who he was dealing with. Her name was Maud Malone. She had been an intercollegiate debater at Radcliffe College, where she graduated summa cum laude. She and Carey Thomas co-founded the National College Equal Suffrage League. Four years before, she led the city's first suffrage parade along Broadway. She was well-known enough that the New York Times included her name in the page-one headline alongside Wilson's in the next day's description of the incident.

Wilson was willing to do nothing about it. After exhausting his repetitive justifications, he slammed the door on the entire situation. "I positively decline to discuss that question now," he informed her and the audience. Wilson then sought to continue with his planned speech as the muscle took over.

Three police officers seized Malone from both the front and behind, tugging her forward and forcing her from behind, causing her to stumble to the ground. At that point, Wilson's campaign secretary stated, "a big detective seized her" and forcibly hauled her out of the auditorium. The well-dressed woman noted for carrying herself "with perfect propriety" was thrown in jail for the night, jewelry included. She was then prosecuted and convicted of disturbing the peace (however, to sidestep the obviously serious First Amendment issues in her case, her conviction was predicated on her reluctance to sit down rather than her speaking up and questioning Wilson). Wilson expressed regret that Malone was dismissed, but insisted that her question was "not pertinent to the national campaign."

Wilson, on the other hand, displayed no signs of humility in the face of his fortuitous election. His early cabinet appointments lent the federal government a distinct political flavor. His initial choice was Bryan, who had been instrumental in his victory at the Baltimore convention and continued to command a loyal following among a significant element of the Democratic base. Wilson did not choose him based on merit. "What use would he be in a Cabinet?" he had questioned Stockbridge during one of their private discussions. "I cannot conceive of him as an administrator of anything." He nonetheless determined that "the place where Bryan can make the least trouble and get the greatest personal glory is as Secretary of State."

His second choice was "Colonel" Edward House, a wealthy Texan he met during the campaign and had grown to trust as an adviser and confidant. He offered House the option of any of the remaining cabinet jobs. House desired a roving commission to weigh in on all issues, so he opted to become, as his biographer puts it, "one of the most powerful Washington insiders in American political history." Without Senate confirmation, he would advise the president on all foreign and domestic issues.

The "colonel" had never served in the military. The title was bestowed upon him by one of the Texas governors he helped put into office. He could also not claim to have any meaningful public administration experience. But his friendship with the president was what was important. The two agreed on almost every political point, from the superiority of the British system of government to issues of race and gender. Wilson later told Dudley Field Malone, "Mr. House is my second personality."

One was Texas Democrat Albert Burleson, an eight-term congressman and House's "closest friends throughout his life." Burleson, like Wilson and House, was the son of a Confederate officer and an ardent segregationist. He had been a floor leader of the Wilson forces at the 1912 convention and chairman of the speakers' bureau during the campaign, and now he was to be postmaster general, a potent position for patronage with more employees than either the Army or the Navy.

Another House recommendation was David Houston, the former president of both Texas A&M and the University of Texas. Both colleges, like Princeton, did refuse black students. Houston would be the House's pick for Agriculture Secretary.

Neither did North Carolinian Josephus Daniels require an introduction. He had been Wilson's publicity director during the presidential campaign, provided editorial support in the Raleigh News & Observer for two years leading up to Wilson's nomination, and even seconded his former Washington correspondent for Wilson's press secretary position.

Dixon was basking in national attention for his election-year novel The Sins of the Father, which attacked interracial marriage, when he submitted this recommendation to the president-elect. It was based on Dixon's play of the same name and became another hit. The book and performance gained national attention despite—or because of—protests from groups such as the Negro Fellowship League, founded by suffragist and civil rights activist Ida Wells-Barnett. In it, Dixon's main character claims that the "negro is the lowest of all human forms." He warns that intermarriage with whites will cause "the degradation of our people to a mongrel negroid level."

Dixon's praise for the president-elect's virtue and how much he would be able to do in office, particularly with the assistance of great men like Josephus Daniels, elicited a gushing response from Wilson. "It is very gratifying to me that you should feel as you do about me," he wrote Dixon from Bermuda on December 3. "And about what there is for me to accomplish." He signed the letter "Faithfully yours, Woodrow Wilson."

To the rest of the country, Wilson's cabinet was noted for its disproportionate representation of southern Democrats. At the time of his swearing-in, the old Confederacy's states accounted for less than a fourth of the total population. Democrats from these eleven states would make up half of Wilson's cabinet—not to mention Colonel House's enormous influence. The Wilson inauguration was about to bring about disastrous changes in the way the executive branch regarded Black people and women thanks to the efforts of these guys.

As the presidential inauguration in March approached, Wilson focused on selecting his administration's senior men. The South may have been the early winner in Wilson's cabinet sweepstakes, but the majority of what was left went to the Northeast, Wilson's main geographical base of support. Only two of the remaining cabinet nominees came from broad areas of the United States that were neither in the South or within 150 miles of New York City Hall.

A particularly important position, secretary to the president, appeared to go to a Northeasterner as well. Wilson briefly considered Josephus Daniels for the top White House position, which is roughly similar to today's White House chief of staff. However, in the months that followed the election, his candidates were reduced to only two. One was Dudley Field Malone, a significant part of Wilson's team during his governorship, the Democratic convention, and the autumn campaign. The other was Joseph Tumulty, a former New Jersey state legislator who appeared to have the inside route, if only because he had served as Wilson's executive secretary throughout his eighteen-month governorship.

Malone had the closest personal relationship with Wilson of the two. He was a frequent Wilson houseguest both before and after the convention, staying at the governor's mansion at Sea Girt and with the governor and his family at Princeton. He and the candidate would take long walks and drive while discussing the campaign. Malone, like McAdoo and Daniels, was a continuous presence at Wilson headquarters, and at the Baltimore convention, he played a critical role in securing votes for Wilson throughout the agonizingly protracted balloting. The New York Times identified Malone and McAdoo as the two New Yorkers who "have rendered yeoman service to Gov. Wilson during the struggle in the convention."

The 1912 election gave Democrats control of both the House and the Senate, and party control over all congressional committees. Because of the Black Codes and Jim Crow, southern Democrats had decades of uninterrupted incumbency, and the informal seniority system on Capitol Hill ensured that they would inherit the majority of those chairmanships. The most senior of them had survived the Republican surge two decades before, following the slump that began with the Panic of 1893.

NAWSA's limited Washington effort had long been led by Elizabeth Kent, who was familiar with congressional lobbying due to her husband, William Kent, a pro-suffrage Republican United States Representative from California. But after Wilson's election, Kent saw little point in continuing to lead the Congressional Committee, as her congressional lobbying campaign was known. Even before the election, her employment had decreased to almost nothing, to the point where she was the sole member of her own "committee." She had grown more unhappy with being a bystander to the biannual routine of introducing the women's suffrage amendment in Congress, with neither the financial resources nor the staff to fight the cause on Capitol Hill.

Shaw understood Kent was keen to move on to more successful ways of pushing the suffrage movement, as prioritized by NAWSA. But she also understood that Kent's yearning to be free of the work was more than equaled by the enthusiasm of two young, aggressive NAWSA members who wanted to take up the job. Lucy Burns and Alice Paul had begged Shaw to put them in Kent's place.

Despite their outstanding credentials, Paul and Burns were not ivory tower scholars. Their political education in the British suffrage movement was honed through experience. They had engaged in civil disobedience as followers of the revolutionary Emmeline Pankhurst and spent time in British jails. They would now base their strategy on Pankhurst's peaceful campaign tactics, such as staging suffrage parades and challenging politicians during public speaking appearances.

Paul and Burns were a whirlwind at the Congressional Committee, turning ideas into action almost rapidly. Before Paul relocated to Washington and established headquarters, the committee had no office at all. The annual budget was 10 dollars. Paul refused to wait for NAWSA's bureaucracy to approve required expenses, so she purchased supplies and rented office space using her own money. The couple chose a strategic position for their command center, directly across the street from the Treasury Department and only two blocks from the White House.

Although the next session of Congress would not begin for another two months, Paul and Burns immediately began developing a thorough plan for influencing important senators and representatives. Simultaneously, to draw national attention to a federal constitutional amendment, they devised even more ambitious plans that extended far beyond their planned meetings on Capitol Hill.

From behind the same desk as Susan B. Anthony, Paul imagined an extravagant, Pankhurst-inspired suffrage parade from the Capitol to the White House. She and Burns planned to gather women from across the country for a large demonstration on the eve of Wilson's inauguration. They had only eight weeks to surpass the formal inaugural procession.

All this was far easier to imagine than to accomplish. Their intentions were seemingly dashed when Richard Sylvester, the chief of the District of Columbia Police, declined to give a permit for a parade from the Capitol to the White House. The grounds he offered for his denial extended beyond the obvious fact that their parade would clash with the official inaugural parade the next day. The larger issue was that, according to the police chief, it was "totally unsuitable for women to be marching down Pennsylvania Avenue."

On March 3, the day before the inauguration, the entire city focused on a march for women's voting rights. The grandstands that had been erected for the official inaugural parade were now full to capacity with both curious and committed spectators. Beyond the filled seats, more onlookers crowded the walkways, bringing the total to almost a quarter million. The pro-suffrage First Lady, Nellie Taft, and her daughter, Helen, had to squeeze past the crowds to reach their private reviewing post.

Fifteen minutes after the parade began, President-elect Woodrow Wilson's train arrived in Washington, D.C. Wilson gazed into the darkness of an almost-empty Union Station, not the crowds of well-wishers he had expected. Aside from the six railroad wagons carrying raucous Princeton undergraduates, hardly no one noticed their arrival. The crowds that had gathered in Washington for the inauguration lined Pennsylvania Avenue to watch the grandiose procession created by Paul & Burns.

The Southern Society was led by a transplanted Virginian who is now one of New York City's prominent Democratic trial lawyers. On the evening of Wilson's speech, a southern Democratic playwright named Augustus Thomas shared the podium with him and the president-elect. Thomas' representations of Black people were well-known for relying heavily on racial stereotypes and comical vernacular. The stag evening's activities recognized divine womanhood and the pinnacle to which women must be elevated. The speakers emphasized the "duty of the men of the party" to lead in politics—and the corresponding obligation of "the women behind them to patiently wait." Wilson's speech on this occasion, reminiscent of his "loving tribute to the virtues of the leaders of secession" at the University of Virginia years earlier, praised the Confederacy's principles and the warriors who fought for "our own way of life."

For a time, the parade ran smoothly and according to plan. But the bars along the parade route were all open, and inside were many males who were opposed to women voting, and their self-control was quickly replaced by alcohol bravery. Crossing the sidewalks to mingle with the marchers, it appeared they may be a little bother, guilty of shouted taunts or a puckish tug on a passing skirt. The provocations swiftly escalated to hair pulling and flag slashing. Many people were terrified when phalanxes of rowdies emerged from the crowd to obstruct the march route and abuse the women. Drunken men and hoodlum youngsters spat at the marchers, grabbed their arms and legs, and threw rocks and bottles. The women in the parade, wearing pennants and respectable attire, were quickly besieged by a "horrible howling mob."

In a controversy that continues to this day, the police did little to quell the subsequent violence. A following congressional investigation revealed significant evidence of police involvement in both physical and verbal abuse of the demonstrators. Police were generally against the suffrage movement. The women were frustrated because the only actual aid they received came from dedicated Boy Scout troops who were considerably outnumbered.

On the morning of his inauguration, Wilson must have been particularly disappointed to see the front page of the Washington Post, where the suffragists were given equal prominence with him. To add salt to injury, he received a personal demand in the form of a telegram from Harriot Stanton Blatch, which was published in the next day's newspapers for all to see. "As you ride today in comfort and safety to the Capitol to be inaugurated," she wrote, please be "mindful that yesterday the Government... left women while passing in a peaceful procession in their demand for political freedom at the mercy of a howling mob."

Blatch pointed out that, in contrast to the lack of protection provided to women, the same parade route on Pennsylvania Avenue would now be "efficiently officered for the protection of men."

Chapter 8: 'A Conviction All My Life'

The stinging defeats on both ends of Pennsylvania Avenue infuriated Alice Paul. She saw the Democrats' arrogance in defeating the federal suffrage amendment as clear evidence of NAWSA's unsuccessful strategy. Within the organization's councils, she had long argued that hedging their bets with a hopelessly Sisyphean state-by-state campaign was a sign of weakness. Now, the group was earning its just reward.

Paul resolved to take matters into her own hands. Since the spring of 1913, she had been expanding the Congressional Committee's reach by establishing a new nationwide auxiliary group, the Congressional Union, which by the end of the year had surpassed a thousand dues-paying members. Its goal was to coordinate grassroots advocacy for the Women's Suffrage Amendment in Congress. Paul seized full control of this new source of funding, bypassing NAWSA's bureaucracy, which she argued was wasting time and money on state-by-state lobbying efforts.

For its part, NAWSA was conflicted between its recent preference for a state-by-state approach and its basic goal of a nationwide amendment. The Democratic argument that suffrage was a states' rights issue encouraged an emphasis on state campaigns. However, NAWSA was under increasing pressure not only from the Congressional Union, but also from other women's organizations, to continue advocating for a constitutional amendment. It had been two years since the National Association of Colored Women's Clubs, led by Mary Church Terrell, declared "in full favor of woman suffrage" across the nation. More recently, the General Federation of Women's Clubs, which has 1.7 million members nationwide, approved the federal amendment at its June 1914 convention in Chicago, providing "immense impetus" to the "passage of the national suffrage amendment," according to Paul.

To demonstrate national support for incorporating women's voting rights into the Constitution, Paul planned for the General Federation of Women's Clubs to send a large delegation to meet with Wilson approximately four months before the midterm elections. On June 30, nearly 500 white-gowned women from every state in the Union assembled in the East Room of the White House. Most people had never been in these amazing surroundings before. Standing beneath the massive Bohemian crystal chandeliers, surrounded by Limoges busts of George Washington, Thomas Jefferson, Abraham Lincoln, and Benjamin Franklin, the delegation's leaders were inspired to speak about democracy. They urged the president to advocate their inclusion. Knowing how he had behaved with prior delegations, they didn't waste much time on pleasantries.

Wilson finally decided he had enough. "I cannot permit myself to be cross-examined," he said, bringing the discussion to a halt. He immediately left the East Room, accompanied by his personal aide and Secret Service guards. The delegates, taken aback by this "astounding arrogance," had been promised the opportunity to stand in single file and be individually presented to the president. "After standing a few minutes gazing at the closed door," the New York Times wrote, "the women slowly filed out."

In the summer of 1914, Alice Paul, Lucy Burns, and their Congressional Union friends concluded that Wilson's continual high-handed rejections should be met by an aggressive campaign to hold him and his party accountable.

At the same time, some NAWSA members drew the opposite inference from the Democratic states' rights blockage of the suffrage amendment, which was imposed on both ends of Pennsylvania Avenue. It conveyed to them that any further resistance was hopeless. Shaw's lieutenants on the newly subdued NAWSA Congressional Committee shared this attitude. Instead of pushing back, they were strengthening their collaboration with Wilson's congressional backers. Setting aside the federal amendment, they attempted to address the states' rights objections through a complicated legislative compromise.

Wilson benefited greatly from the Shafroth-Palmer substitution. First, it would invalidate the federal suffrage amendment. Second, it provided political cover for senators and congressmen who claimed to be working for suffrage but accomplished little or nothing. Third, it made no provision for federal enforcement, leaving each state free to define its own electorate, thereby protecting Jim Crow throughout the South.

Because Shafroth-Palmer was a proposed constitutional amendment, the new NAWSA-backed alternative would be just as difficult to pass as the women's suffrage amendment. It would need to be passed by supermajorities in both chambers of Congress. Then it would need to be approved by at least three-quarters of state legislatures. Years may pass before these processes can be completed. Even if all this had been done, no woman would have received the vote.

Instead, suffrage campaigners in each state would need to collect signatures from 8% of the men who voted in the last election. Once this was completed, they would need to acquire funds and launch a statewide initiative campaign in each state where women were unable to vote. In short, it was the same state-by-state grind that had dominated the previous half-century. Wilson's long-awaited second term would be a distant memory by the time anything tangible could be created via this arduous path.

It appears unlikely that NAWSA became involved in this diversion in the first place. At the group's 1914 convention in Nashville, the new leadership of NAWSA's Congressional Committee openly revealed their decision to withdraw from a federal amendment as an effort to please racist senators. The committee's lobbyists had canvassed numerous senators about their positions on the federal amendment and discovered that "the race question" was the sticking point. According to the information gathered, the objecting senators would be most comfortable if they could utilize the states' rights argument to avoid the issue of Black women voting. It was thus by purpose that the Shafroth-Palmer amendment, NAWSA's attempt to achieve this goal, was both unprincipled and ineffectual.

On August 5, 1914, Senator Shafroth focused his attention on a completely other issue: the financial crisis in the United States caused by the commencement of war in Europe. That morning, four-inch-tall headlines trumpeted England's declaration of war on Germany. At the request of Treasury Secretary McAdoo, Secretary of State Bryan, and Secretary of War Garrison, Shafroth announced on the Senate floor the limited conditions under which Americans could ship gold to

Europe "for the relief of distress." In recent weeks, as Europeans desperately liquidated their U.S. securities holdings and gold outflows soared, stock prices fell so sharply that the New York Stock Exchange halted trading indefinitely. The nation's banking and financial systems appeared to be on the edge of collapse.

From the White House, Wilson issued a warning against panic. However, the financial disaster was not the only crisis he and the country faced. Following his August 4 proclamation of strict American neutrality, he addressed another emergency: tens of thousands of Americans stranded in Europe with no money, food, or a way out. Maintaining the president's own calm required superhuman effort—not least because upstairs in the executive residence, his wife, Ellen, lay suffering in the room where she had been confined since shortly after their daughter Eleanor's wedding to Treasury Secretary William McAdoo on May 7.

Around midday the next day, one of the attending physicians gave Ellen the grim news that she just had hours to survive. The sun had not fallen when she breathed her last. The president was holding her hand as she died.

Condolences were sent from around the world. Austria-Hungary lowered its flags to half-mast during the war. NAWSA eulogized the First Lady's death, stating that it invoked the sorrow and sympathy "of all the people"—"even amid the grief over the terrible war in Europe."

Wilson was practically paralyzed by grief for months, sinking into a dark depression. Two weeks after Ellen's funeral, he declared himself "exhausted,—dead in heart and body, weighed down with a leaden indifference and despair." In late August, he informed Colonel House that "there was nothing left in him worthwhile." By November, he had little emotional progress. He still complained that he "had no heart in the things he was doing." He admitted to Colonel House, not for the first time, that he wished "someone would kill him."

The influence of the Congressional Union campaign in every state where women already had the right to vote was a wild card, explaining why President Wilson and the Democratic caucuses in both the House and Senate opposed the federal amendment. The campaign asked female voters to send a message by voting Democrats up and down the ballot. In a perspective on the 1914 election, Paul lieutenant Florence Brewer Boeckel noted that their message to voters was obvious. "Do not use your votes to send back to power the party that has... opposed the freedom of women at every turn." Women, they said, must "recognize and acknowledge that they have an enemy, the Democratic Party."

When the ballots were tabulated after the midterm elections, the Democrats had narrowly retained control of Congress—albeit only in the House. Republicans won sixty-two House seats, almost enough for a majority. The House Democratic leadership undoubtedly felt the sting of the Congressional Union's campaign barbs, even though, without exit polls at the time, it was difficult to determine the precise impact of its pro-suffrage, anti-Democrat message on the overall outcome.

What should have concerned party leaders the most was that the Congressional Union had caused all of these problems with just two field members in each suffrage state, and occasionally only one. Paul made it obvious that her low-budget 1914 campaign was only a test run. If Wilson and his party failed to pass the women's suffrage amendment again, Paul declared that the Congressional Union would campaign against Democrats in every state. She vowed that with two years to plan, the next campaign would be far better funded.

Trotter reminded the president that black voters had "made plain enough to you their opposition to segregation last year by a national anti-segregation petition," which he had personally delivered to Wilson in the White House. These voters had now spoken more clearly, "by a protest registered at the polls, voting against every Democratic candidate save those outspoken against segregation."

Trotter stood his ground. "For fifty years, white and colored clerks have been working together in peace and harmony and friendliness," he told Wilson, up until "your inauguration."

Rather than make amends with his steadfast former supporter, Wilson dug in. "Segregation of white and negro civil service employees," he told reporters, "is to be continued." This unqualified presidential proclamation would be front-page news in the next day's New York Times.

Undaunted, Trotter persisted. Trotter reminded Wilson that four of his Republican predecessors had chosen Black men as Registers of the Treasury, an important job that involves signing every piece of US paper currency. Wilson had considered selecting Adam Patterson, a Black man, but opted to break with a thirty-year tradition when southern Democratic senators opposed on racial grounds. Despite getting McAdoo's personal assurance that he had "spoken with each of the Senators about [Patterson], and they approve his appointment," Wilson withdrew the nomination just days after announcing it.

Trotter had no idea how bad the situation really was. Wilson explained it in private correspondence with Thomas Dixon. The president said the only reason he considered choosing Patterson to manage this Treasury office was because he had previously segregated it. That way, there would be no "Negro men over white women employees of the Treasury Department," as Dixon had alleged to Wilson. The president informed Dixon that he had "a plan of concentration" that would group all Black federal employees together and would not mix the two races in any one bureau. This change has already taken effect in the bureau to which I proposed Patterson's appointment."

It dashed Trotter's and other civil rights activists' hopes for Wilson. Despite his socialist leanings, Trotter would back Republican Charles Evans Hughes in the next presidential race.

Following the meeting, Wilson commiserate with his fellow segregationist, Josephus Daniels. "I was damn fool enough," he said, "to lose my cool and point them to the door. What I should have done," he told Daniels, "was to assure them that their petition would, of course, be considered. They would have then quietly withdrawn, and nothing more would have been heard of the situation."

If Wilson, in his depressed mood, was unconcerned about previous and future elections, senators and representatives on Capitol Hill were not. The Democratic leadership publicly asserted that the midterm results had left them unimpressed. Privately, Champ Clark, the Democratic Speaker of the House who had supported women's suffrage before being elected to Congress, was concerned about the ramifications of leading a party that was overwhelmingly opposed.

The referendum was slated for mid-January, giving proponents for women's suffrage only a few weeks to rally support. Short of a presidential endorsement, it appeared that little could be done to move enough Democratic votes to attain the required two-thirds majority. As a result, NAWSA's Congressional Union sent a politically friendly delegation of Democratic women to the White House for an urgent meeting.

On Tuesday, January 12, 1915, the House began debate on the federal suffrage amendment. It was the same language that had been introduced in every Congress since Senator Aaron Sargent first proposed it nearly four decades ago. The rule governing debate allotted six hours of floor time, plus an hour and a half for the formality of discussing the rule. This was a hefty allocation suitable for a serious piece of legislation. But Democratic leaders had simply agreed to facilitate the vote. They had made no promises about how they would vote.

After all, Representative Frank Mondell of Wyoming, a Republican, pushed the suffrage amendment. Throughout the argument, Democratic delegates referenced their prior caucus vote against the women's suffrage amendment as conclusive, implying that the outcome of the next roll call vote was predetermined.

He then referenced what he saw as the bad experience of enabling Black men to vote. "At one time in my own State [that is, after the 15th Amendment, and before the end of Reconstruction] universal manhood suffrage was granted to the people of Alabama," the speaker of the legislature grumbled. The "portion of my State that suffered the worst were the good women and children." That is why, he stated, "this question must be settled by the individual states."

Democratic House members repeated the majority leader's comments, extolling the virtues of chivalry and feminine purity before finishing with the inviolability of states' rights. "Mr. Speaker," Georgia representative Charles Bartlett said, "we attempted to impose universal suffrage on the States in the division from which I belong.

When we enfranchised the black male, there was disorder, mayhem, criminality, and a nightmare. He claimed that enfranchising Black women would be much more harmful because "the black female was worse in her antagonism to the white race than the black male."

The House debate over the suffrage amendment lasted into the night. Finally, Frank Mondell spoke for the Republicans. He addressed the Democratic leader's racist argument front on. He stated that to guarantee Black men's voting rights, the 15th Amendment had to be "shot into the Constitution." In contrast, this was an opportunity to effect constitutional change to expand voting rights "in a peaceful and orderly manner." It was a not-so-subtle reminder that the debate over civil rights vs state rights was settled at the point of a bayonet when the Union won the Civil War.

Suffragists might take heart from the 174-204 vote, which put them within sixteen votes of an overwhelming majority of the House in favor. However, the actual takeaway from the day's debate and voting was that much more work would be required to gain the two-thirds support needed for a constitutional change.

Shortly after the women's suffrage amendment was defeated in the House, NAWSA president Anna Howard Shaw requested and received a meeting with the president. Given his repeated resistance, she did not even attempt to request his approval for the amendment. Instead, because Wilson "consistently maintained and reiterated his attitude" that women's suffrage was "a matter for the states," Shaw merely inquired if he would support the women's suffrage initiative that was currently pending in his home state of New Jersey.

Even when asked, Wilson declined to express his support for women's suffrage.

At least he would not express his opinion in public. In private at the White House, he freely stated his view that granting women the right to vote, whether through state or federal action, would have negative effects for the nation's social fabric while making "absolutely no change in politics." At breakfast the morning of his appointment with Shaw, Wilson discussed his upcoming meeting with the NAWSA president and used the occasion to rant. According to Nancy Saunders

Toy, the president's houseguest at the table, if women get the vote, "it is the home that will be disastrously affected." After all, housework must be done, "and who is going to do it if the women won't?" Toy, the wife of a Harvard professor and a longtime Wilson family friend, put the president's statements in quotes in her diary. On the day of his encounter with Shaw, he expressed his opinion as follows.

While Wilson's goal was to avoid criticism by remaining silent on the issue and, when appropriate, using his states' rights mantra, his now-very public position opposing a federal amendment placed him solidly in the "anti" category. The National Association Opposed to Woman Suffrage enthusiastically endorsed the president's recent public statement that "the woman suffrage question can be solved most solidly and conclusively' by the states." Wilson's viewpoint, they said in 1915, "is exactly what anti-suffragists believe!"

Chapter 9: 'A Towering Rage'

In December 1915, Wilson was once again beset with calls to include a word in support of women's suffrage in his State of the Union address. He turned them down. Interestingly, he scheduled White House meetings with NAWSA and its adversary, the National Association Opposed to Woman Suffrage, on the same day. The "antis," whom Wilson praised as "most gracious ladies," had arrived "to thank him for his announced opposition to a federal suffrage amendment." Carrie Chapman Catt of NAWSA probably had Wilson in mind when she told the House Judiciary Committee on December 16 that "when a man believes in woman suffrage, it is a national question, and when he does not believe in it, he says it is a question for the states."

NAWSA was easier to deal with, but their findings were identical. With the Democratic National Convention less than two months away, they differentially proposed numerous wordings for a suffrage plank in the party platform, none of which included approval of the Anthony Amendment. Wilson signed off on a section that vaguely mentioned "enfranchisement" without describing how it could be accomplished.

For five weeks in April and May, the Congressional Union continued the pressure on with a splashy "Suffrage Special" train trip of the West, featuring famous speakers advocating for the Anthony Amendment. The 8,000-mile whistle-stop campaign thrilled audiences in Illinois, Kansas, Wyoming, Colorado, Arizona, California, Nevada, Oregon, Washington, Montana, Idaho, Utah, and Missouri, earning governors and mayors' support along the way. The rolling publicity tour not only kept suffrage in the spotlight, but it also promoted Alice Paul's latest project, the forthcoming Chicago conference of the new National Woman's Party.For her part, Alice Paul found it amusing that Malone "became absolutely furious, furious that we would dream of opposing the Democrats." Of course, we opposed the Democrats, she explained, since "they were opposing us." But Malone wouldn't give up. He would have "stood there and argued on that platform," Paul later said, until hotel management came "and put down the curtain to send him home." His clear irritation was that he could not provide a firm promise that Wilson or the Democratic Party would change their policies. "That was the reason," Paul explained, "why he was in such a rage."

On June 7, the Republican National Convention began at the Chicago Coliseum, following the conclusion of the National Woman's Party convention. Charles Evans Hughes, former New York governor and incumbent Supreme Court justice, would be nominated shortly by the newly united GOP. Their theme was "preparedness," and it would be carried out by a procession of speakers who promised to speedily construct an armed force that Germany would not dare to challenge. But the Chicago Tribune headlines that hailed the Republicans' arrival read "SUFFRAGE AND PREPAREDNESS," providing just as much press to the National Woman's Party and its demands for the Anthony Amendment.

Sticking to that message was difficult. Within days of his nomination, Wilson earned unpleasant news for his contact with a Virginia Federation of Labor delegate, to whom he had granted a White House meeting without learning she was there to present him with the union's resolutions calling for action on the Anthony Amendment. "I am opposed to conviction and political traditions," he explained simply. That emphasized the Democratic platform's desire for suffrage to be established "by the states."

Wilson's anti-amendment beliefs made headlines again a week later, when a member of a Democratic Party support organization confronted him at a White House meeting. You have "no right to pledge the support of the Democratic women of the country" for your efforts, she informed a surprised Wilson, because millions of women "regard you as having been responsible for the defeat of the woman suffrage amendment." She continued in this vein for five minutes— "long enough to drive home her points," according to the New York Times. Wilson had another opportunity to make his point. "Women should be patient," he told her.

On July 5, she emailed the plan to NAWSA president Carrie Chapman Catt, who had reason to be concerned. Thomas was well-known then. She was one of the movement's venerable leaders, serving as the founding president of the National College Equal Suffrage League just shy of her 60th birthday. She had known the late Susan B. Anthony as a friend and had hosted her several times. During Emmeline Pankhurst's 1911 NAWSA conference in Kentucky, she personally welcomed the British suffrage leader on her American tour. She was also an effective fundraiser: she co-led the Susan B. Anthony Memorial Fund with her companion, Mary Garrett, and contributed significant sums to NAWSA.

The second half of Thomas' plan focused on Wilson. She was aware that her previous charge at Bryn Mawr lacked any personal conviction in support of women's suffrage. She reasoned that he could only be forced to modify his opinion on the Anthony Amendment due to political necessity. Catt should question Hughes about NAWSA's decision to endorse him, "unless he will come out for the federal amendment and pass it through this Congress."

Thomas had a strong appreciation for what made Wilson tick. She understood his views on women, which she despised, and his racial intolerance, which she shared. Above all, she recognized that, despite Wilson's lofty speech, he was deeply political. As she now emphasized to Catt, Wilson's primary interest at the moment was his own reelection. He would support the Anthony Amendment if he felt it was required for his survival.

The discriminating woman who had known Woodrow Wilson for over thirty years presented a convincing case. Anna Howard Shaw, Catt's predecessor as NAWSA president, agreed with Thomas and recommended this technique.

Catt initially met Hughes, as advised by Thomas. But Alice Paul had arrived first. The Republican nominee had promptly responded to her urgent plea to see him.

They met the day after the Fourth of July, the same day Thomas revealed her plan to Catt. Paul discovered Hughes in his eighth-floor campaign suite at the Hotel Astor, still in the process of relocating from Washington to New York, setting up an office, and hiring his first staff. This devotion to Alice Paul represented more than Hughes' support for women's suffrage. It also represented his belief that she was a political force to be reckoned with.

Such blunt talk would have angered Wilson, as it did on previous occasions. But Hughes reacted differently. The previous New York governor has thicker skin than the current president. He was also at ease with women in business, academia, and politics, and Paul herself, because he was ready to offer what she sought.

Paul exited the meeting satisfied that she had received her desired outcome. As she and Carpenter walked out of the hotel, passing through four massive paintings depicting New York's progress from "Ancient to Modern," they brought with them the Republican nominee's commitment to assist American women overcome ancient barriers to participation in modern life. Hughes informed them he would support the Anthony amendment. He planned to announce it to the public soon after his acceptance speech, which was slated for the end of the month.

Two weeks later, NAWSA representatives Catt and Shaw visited Hughes headquarters. Vira Boarman Whitehouse, the chairwoman of the New York State Woman Suffrage Party and the campaign's leader for state suffrage joined them. Hughes also guaranteed his support for the Anthony Amendment to these three women, requesting that they keep the news hidden until his planned announcement date. They immediately agreed during a chat that NAWSA described as "long and satisfactory." The NAWSA officials were clearly thrilled with the candidate's support for the Anthony Amendment, calling it "most gratifying."

But at this point, Catt deviated from Carey Thomas' plan. Instead of offering Hughes NAWSA's conditional support, she and her colleagues simply thanked him. Susan B. Anthony had urged the organization "to give aid and comfort to any party which shall inscribe on its banners 'Freedom to Women,'" Catt put Hughes on ice while preparing to give Wilson another opportunity. On July 27, Catt and Jennie Bradley Roessing, the new chair of NAWSA's Congressional Committee, requested a meeting with the president.

According to Blatch's version of the conversation, he "exploded" the notion that state rights were the reason he opposed the Anthony Amendment. Five years ago, he told his publicity director Frank Stockbridge that the states' rights argument was nothing more than a ruse. "Dismiss from your minds the idea that my party or I are concerned about states' rights," Wilson warned her. "It is the negro question, Mrs. Blatch, that keeps my party from doing as you wish."

Blatch would not let it go at that. She chose to debate him on his own terms. If all women were allowed to vote, she responded, "the proportion of white to black voters" would not change. Wilson only grinned before correcting her "in a very low voice." "In two states," he explained, "the blacks would still be preponderate." Not unexpectedly, the president was well-versed in the South's racial demographics. He was referring to South Carolina and Mississippi, which both had Black populations over 55 percent.

As expected, Hughes' speech contained an endorsement of women's voting rights. On July 31, with Republican supporters filling all three thousand seats in Carnegie Hall, the recently retired Supreme Court justice reaffirmed his support for women's suffrage without delay. He mocked those who stood in the way, saying they "cannot defeat this movement." Any additional stalling would cause "a bitter struggle," hurting the country's overall welfare. Hughes emphasized that, for the sake of the country, "the contest should be ended promptly." This implied a federal solution rather than the glacial, state-by-state process. However, Hughes failed to make that point obvious in a speech that covered a wide range of topics, including the federal budget, war, and peace. Was he or was he not endorsing the Anthony Amendment, as he had promised Paul and Catt weeks ago?

He dispelled all doubts the next day at an event completely dedicated to his endorsement. Hughes enthusiastically supported the Anthony Amendment in front of a crowd of about 500 ladies at the Hotel Astor's Grand Ballroom, which was appropriately flanked by larger-than-life caryatid maidens supporting the massive arched roof. He made it obvious that if it were up to President Hughes, the protracted fight for the vote, which began in earnest with the Seneca Falls conference sixty-eight years ago, would be easily won. The suffrage issue was one that "should be promptly settled" for "the whole country." He desired that the Anthony Amendment be "submitted and ratified, and the subject removed from political discussion," and he "would take the shortest cut" to accomplish this. Failure to act quickly presented a threat "to our security, unity, and proper attitude toward political questions."

The Hughes announcement put Wilson under great pressure to go beyond his states' rights stance. Alice Paul pointed out that it "leaves the Democrats in an embarrassing solitude of opposition," as not only the Republicans and Progressives, but also "the National Prohibition and Socialist parties have already declared for the amendment." Catt, who had now abandoned Thomas's proposal entirely, did not exert any pressure on Wilson during their meeting. She and her subordinate, Roessing, were friendly, making no mention of leveraging their organization's national clout against him in the 1916 presidential election.

As expected, the visit yielded no results. According to the official NAWSA version of the meeting, both women respectfully acknowledged Wilson's latest rejection of the Anthony amendment. "We presented the arguments on behalf of the Federal Amendment," their report reads, "but he remained unconvinced."

The fact that the president was unaffected by Hughes or NAWSA quickly became apparent. "Wilson Unchanged on Suffrage Issue," read the front-page headline in the New York Times the day after his meeting with Catt. He has "not changed his mind," according to a White House statement, "notwithstanding Charles E. Hughes' declaration in favor of the Federal amendment." Both Vice President Marshall and Colonel House advocated for keeping the course. Marshall instructed him to avoid addressing women's voting rights during the campaign. House anticipated that Hughes' support for the Anthony Amendment "would cost him the election, if nothing else did."

Wilson wrote two personal letters that week, which provide insight into his thinking. One was addressed to a family friend, a "born suffragist" who had urged him to support the Anthony Amendment. The other was to the wife of a Princeton trustee, who, like her husband, was a fervent anti-suffragist, and had written to him to endorse his states' rights attitude.

Wilson reassured his pro-suffrage acquaintance that she should "not for a moment doubt the sincerity of my belief in the principle of woman suffrage," but then categorically rejected the Anthony Amendment. "I would a great deal rather have the respect of the women than their votes," he asserted, stressing that his "attitude in this matter has again and again been very frankly avowed." He thanked his anti-suffrage friend for her confidence in him. He told her he would not budge. He promised her that his "convictions on the suffrage question were well-formed."

Part III: Holding Back the Tide
Chapter 10: The 'Firm Hand of Stern Repression'

Since 1788, when Congress set the date for George Washington to take the oath, presidents have been sworn in March 4th. On the three previous occasions in the country's history when Inauguration Day fell on a Sunday, the presidents rescheduled their swearing-in to the day before or following. In 1917, Wilson elected to be the first to take the oath of office on Sunday, albeit he did so privately before the official event the next day.

This particular Sunday in March was cold, dismal, and rainy, so Wilson's ceremonies were held quietly inside. The majestic presidential Pierce-Arrow drove gently on the slippery asphalt as Harry and Edith slowly made their way up Pennsylvania Avenue to the Capitol, arriving slightly battered at the President's Room on the north side of the Senate chamber. Cabinet and a few friends greeted them. At noon, Chief Justice Edward White was to take the oath.

Now White recounted the words from the Constitution and requested Wilson to repeat them. Edith proudly stood behind her spouse of less than 14 months. Wilson stood in front of his own pro-segregation cabinet, surrounded by finely framed photographs of George Washington and the members of the first cabinet, and solemnly read the oath with his hand on the Bible. He then bent to kiss the holy book, just as Washington had done.

As the afternoon progressed, the president worked at his desk, writing an indictment of the "helpless and contemptible" legislative branch. The clatter of his keyboard echoed the sounds of freezing rain hitting the adjoining window panes. Soon, the rat-a-tat-tat of a snare drum joined the clamor, matching the iconic strains of "The Battle Hymn of the Republic," which suffragist composer Wilson had spied on from the rafters in Baltimore years earlier. During the third month of silent sentinels picketing, the National Woman's Party organized a "monster picket" for his inauguration. The approximately 1,000 marchers outside his windows circled the White House to the tempo of "Onward, Christian Soldiers" and "La Marseillaise," attracting many more spectators despite the weather. The women's brigades, with their brass bands and banners, were a sight to behold.

Despite Dudley Field Malone's personal plea that they be permitted to give their resolutions to the president, the women were turned away at each gate, held back by "almost as many police officers as marchers." The White House was ready for them, but not in the way they had expected. For over two hours, they persisted. They refused to give up, despite being thoroughly soaked and chilled to the bone. Some were as old as 84. They would see the president.

Finally, the gates to the White House opened. However, the women were not allowed in. It was to let Wilson out. His limousine cut over the picket line, drenching the women on both sides. Doris Stevens stated that when the First Lady sat next to him, the president "looked straight ahead as if [we] were invisible." At that point, she claimed, "the weary marchers realized that President Wilson had deliberately turned them away."

As Wilson disappeared along Pennsylvania Avenue into the rain, Jeannette Rankin was working her way up the Eastern Seaboard.

The recently elected representative from Montana, who will soon become the first woman to serve in Congress, was on a constant press tour, with over twenty speaking engagements scheduled ahead of the start of Congress on April 2. Moviegoers across the country tracked her travels with Hearst-Pathé newsreels that documented the ecstatic audiences at each site. Her celebrity grew with each shot, and the famous and powerful were always present to greet her.

Until she came, the cause of women's votes remained an abstraction in the Capitol's all-male hallways. However, under the rules of both chambers, Congresswoman Rankin was now free to come and go as she pleased in this most sacred of male redoubts. Her privileges as a House member included the ability to stroll directly onto the Senate floor—and when she first did so, staying for several hours during discussion, it "created a mild sensation." Men were regularly astonished to see a woman walking the marble-pillared corridors of the Capitol's closed-to-the-public rooms.

On the first day of the extraordinary session of Congress convened to debate the United States' involvement in the war, the NWP moved their pickets from the White House to Capitol Hill. As Rankin traversed the huge plaza on the east front of the Capitol to ascend the marble stairs to the House chamber, she smiled at the quiet sentinels who stood guard. Their gold banners indicated that Britain, like Russia's interim government under Prince Georgy Lvov, was providing women the right to vote throughout the war. "How long," their letter asked, reinforcing Wilson's unwanted advice, "must American women wait for their liberty?"

Rankin's ceremonial introduction to Congress was spectacular. Her home-state colleague, a Democrat, escorted her to the floor in the most gracious manner possible. "The men were clapping and cheering around her on both sides of the aisle." The former NAWSA lobbyist held a bouquet in the National Woman's Party's purple and gold colors, indicating her sympathies for the opposing suffragist factions. When she went to take her seat further back on the Republican side, she was unable to do so until almost every member had shaken her hand.

The first vote of the first woman in Congress was to install Republican leader James Mann as Speaker (albeit the Democrats had partnered with Socialist and Progressive members of the House to assure Champ Clark's reelection). According to custom, the vote for Speaker is viva voce—live voice voting. So, when the clerk shouted her name again, she responded loudly: "Mann!" And, as before, there was an outburst of cheering, but this time just from the Republican side of the aisle.

That day, she introduced the first bill she would sponsor. It was the Susan B. Anthony Amendment, as proposed by Senator Aaron Sargent in 1878.

Regardless of partisan politics, Jeannette Rankin had established herself. There was more to come on her historic first day. That evening, the House chamber will hold a joint session of Congress, during which Wilson would request a formal declaration of war against Germany.

He attacked Germany's despotism while hailing Russia's czar's abdication. "Does not every American," he lamented, "feel that assurance has been added to our hope for the future peace of the world by the wonderful and heartening things that have been happening within the last few weeks in Russia?" It was the worst foreign policy prediction of the twentieth century, coming a month after the establishment of the Petrograd Soviet and just days before Lenin climbed atop a train car at Finland Station in the Russian capital and ignited the Bolshevik-led Russian Civil War, shouting to the crowd,

"Long live the worldwide Socialist revolution!"

Wilson's transition from peace candidate to war president was startlingly quick. Only three weeks had passed between his inauguration and his war speech. Throughout most of that time, even as public opinion shifted gradually in favor of war, his public statements remained noncommittal. The White House pattern appeared to have remained constant, as he continued to play golf every day, even the day of his war message.

The shift in popular opinion began before the November election, as indicated by the development of enormous "preparedness" parades in cities around the country. Daily news stories of death and misery in Europe, papal appeals on behalf of war-victimized children, and the sentiments of millions of immigrants with deep ties to the several fighting nations pushed Americans to choose sides. Both the Allies and the Central Powers used propaganda to try to influence public opinion in the United States, although Britain had a clear advantage due to its better ability to produce English-language content.

Many believed American national pride was on the line. Years of well-publicized indignities, such as the sinking of the Lusitania, the discovery of German saboteurs in the northeastern United States, and, most recently, the notorious Zimmermann telegram, conveying Germany's secret invitation to Mexico to join the Central Powers in war against the United States in exchange for financial and diplomatic support for Mexico's reconquest of Texas, New Mexico, and Arizona, fueled public outrage.

Wilson's power over the D.C. government was legal and personal. Federal law required that one of the three D.C. commissioners be from the Army Corps of Engineers, but he filled the other two positions with close friends. One was Oliver Peck Newman, the former top editorial writer for the Washington Times, who had been assigned by the Scripps and United Press syndicates to accompany Wilson during the 1912 campaign. Newman followed Wilson until Inauguration Day, and even accompanied him on his post-election trip. All the while, he wrote positive tales about the candidate.

Wilson's other political appointee was Louis Brownlow, an equally favorable journalist who, like the president, was the son of a Confederate officer and formerly owned slaves. Brownlow was a fan and acquaintance of Wilson's supremacist professor, Richard T. Ely. As a young man, he excitedly read Wilson's Atlantic Monthly pieces denouncing Reconstruction. I "cannot even pretend," Brownlow said years later in his retirement, "that I then escaped the heritage of race prejudice." Like Wilson, he believed that his "southern, Confederate, Democratic family" had given him a "tolerant outlook" in his "relations with Negroes."

Brownlow was editor of three separate Kentucky newspapers. As state political editor for the Nashville Banner, he hired and mentored Wilson's brother, Joe. Brownlow and the then-president of Princeton had "several long talks" at the time, which formed the foundation of his decades-long connection with his current boss. When Brownlow moved north to become the Nashville Banner's Washington reporter, Oliver Newman became his "very closest friend." Soon after, Wilson named them both to the D.C. Board of Commissioners.

Wilson wielded unrivalled power to stifle dissent in the nation's capital, thanks to his specific legal authority and strong ties with these appointments. He began using it more often.

Representative Rankin sensed a hostile attitude for war doubters in the Capitol right away. It was obvious to her that individuals who questioned the Wilson administration's war plans were judged guilty of "cowardice and disloyalty." Even at that early stage, she wrote to a Republican colleague, Karl Stefan of Nebraska, after the war, "knew that none of the idealistic hopes would be carried out."

It would be three more days till she had to vote yes or no on the war. But meanwhile, she had her own urgent priority: the Anthony Amendment. Rankin spoke with James Mann, the House minority leader who led Republicans to vote overwhelmingly for the Anthony Amendment two years ago. Mann's cooperation allowed her to be put ahead of her more senior colleagues as the lead sponsor of House Joint Resolution 3. In a letter to a friend, she stated that he "told me that he would do all he could to help me with the suffrage amendment." Mann later told her, "You and I will carry out this woman's suffrage."

When it came to strategizing on the Anthony Amendment, Rankin felt more at ease with Mann than with NAWSA executives. He collaborated with both the NWP and NAWSA, as she did, and was more concerned with results than which organization believed it was in command. He had long been involved with the Chicago Equal Suffrage Association in his home state, where women were granted the right to vote in presidential elections in 1913. A year after convincing more than two-thirds of House Republicans to support the Anthony Amendment in 1915, he appeared in Chicago with Elizabeth Bass of the Democratic National Committee to promote the amendment.

To make matters worse, Shaw's letter was more concerned with Rankin's impending war vote than the Anthony Amendment. Because NAWSA had fully committed to war, they expected Rankin to do the same. This demand for uniformity on non-suffrage policies, coming from an organization dedicated to women's freedom to fully engage as individual citizens in politics, exacerbated the difficulty of her life-or-death decision.

Carter Glass, an anti-suffrage and pro-Jim Crow representative from Virginia, insisted on bringing the moratorium motion before the Democratic Caucus. He would soon take over as vice president of the Woman Patriot Publishing Company in Washington, D.C., which publishes the National Association Opposed to Woman Suffrage's official journal.

The Glass resolution provided political cover for Democrats caught in the crossfire over women's suffrage and a number of other contentious issues, most notably prohibition. It was a simple method for the ruling party to postpone what would almost certainly be unpopular votes among many of its members. Only if the president himself wrapped an issue in the flag would they be forced to vote on it—and then they might use the exigencies of war as justification, as they would soon do with the prohibition of alcoholic beverages.

Anti-suffrage groups overwhelmingly backed the moratorium, mocking the notion that a constitutional change granting women's voting rights could be considered a war measure. Having previously highlighted Rankin's vote against the war as proof that suffragists "have no patriotism," they now hailed Wilson's war policy even louder since, as implemented by the congressional leadership, it appeared to be a wonderful strategy to hog-tie the Anthony Amendment.

Chapter 11: 'Lock Them Up'

This paradigm of concision, a scant seventy-nine words, set off the tornado. The CPI, or Creel Committee, as it was often dubbed after its chairman, swiftly evolved into a massive bureaucracy manned by over 150,000 ex-journalists, press agents, Hollywood filmmakers, stump speeches, and politicians with broad powers. Wilson's actions in developing this extraordinary machinery demonstrated his desire to silence "unpatriotic" voices critical of his policies. The year before, he had only held two press conferences. He was no longer satisfied with avoiding challenging questions; instead, he would resort to news manipulation.

Even during peacetime, Wilson lobbied Congress for explicit media censorship powers. Addressing a joint assembly in 1915, more than a year before reconsidering his stance of not participating in the war, he advocated for laws granting him power over any public utterance that sought to "bring the authority and good name of our Government into contempt." Since Congress had not yet given him what he desired, he decided to act unilaterally.

As early as 1905, he penned an editorial supporting Wilson for President. During the 1912 campaign, he created a Wilson club in Denver and met with the candidate for an hour during his fall visit. Following the 1912 election, the two initiated a personal communication in which Creel displayed his allegiance and willingness to serve in the administration. After his reelection, Wilson boasted that his glowing syndicated news pieces played "a rather important part in the 1916 campaign."

Following the April 6 war declaration, Creel read in the media that Wilson intended to establish a censorship agency, so he promptly developed a proposal for an international propaganda operation and sent it to the White House. Wilson summoned him to a meeting.

Creel, like Wilson, the son of a Confederate officer, agreed with the president on nearly every topic of the day. Creel's signature style, however, was to cast all players in black and white. "To Creel, there are only two classes of men," said Collier's Weekly, "skunks, and the greatest man that ever lived." According to the CPI, Wilson would presently be considered the greatest guy.

Creel and Wilson did, however, have a significant disagreement on one issue: women's voting rights.

The two men did discuss a media "campaign" that would reach "not only the United States, but every neutral country, and also into England, France, and Italy." The emphasis would be on creating news rather than simply repressing expression. "As for censorship," Creel told me, "all proper needs could be met by some voluntary methods." That is, the new organization would compel editors to censor themselves.

The New York Times noted his "publicly expressed hostility toward certain newspapers," which is particularly concerning given his "position of authority over the press." No newspaper or magazine wanted to be on the losing end of his "friend-foe public polemics," as University of Maryland professor Jonathan Auerbach called Creel's one-sided attacks. Auerbach noted that he was motivated "more by militant emotional animus than by attempts to persuade via rational argument." Creel may not have been "a fascist," Auerbach continued, but his use of journalism and propaganda "carried certain absolutist tendencies."

The initial focus was on crushing opposition to the new conscription law, which Wilson signed on May 18 after just 73,000 volunteers enlisted. The Selective Service Act, the first draft since the Civil War, sparked intense debate in Congress, with Speaker of the House Champ Clark leading the opposition. Now the law of the land, it would soon enlist more than 2.8 million men in the armed forces. Wilson, the historian, was well aware of the conscription riots that had erupted the previous time this was done, during the Civil War, and both he and his government desired to prevent such disturbances. One approach to accomplish this was to limit public debate about the draft.

In the months that followed, when suffragists pointed out the obvious contradiction between Wilson's lofty democracy rhetoric and his opposition to the Anthony Amendment, not only the new wartime communications bureau but Wilson himself intervened to restrict coverage of their demonstrations. Creel and his army of propagandists allegedly supported the war effort by condemning suffragists who challenged the president as disloyal foes of the Allied cause.

The volunteers of the National Woman's Party, knowing their intentions were genuine, continued to mock Wilson's pro-democracy rhetoric and happily accepted the repercussions. They were anxious to use Wilson's remarks on their flags, as they did on April 23, when Britain's foreign secretary, Arthur Balfour, arrived at the White House with a large delegation for a meeting on war strategy. Balfour, a former British prime minister, was unconcerned, having previously opted to support his country's suffragists. He was known to wear their colors in solidarity whenever he passed by similar votes-for-women protests outside Downing Street. Wilson's war speech expressed America's commitment to fighting for the right of individuals who submit to authority to have a role in their own governments. This effectively expressed the suffragists' own goal.

In a further effort to appease his questioners, Wilson stated that he had written the Democratic chairman of the House Rules Committee in support of establishing a House counterpart to the Senate Select Committee on Woman Suffrage. He didn't mention that NAWSA had asked him to do so, and that he was delighted to divert attention away from himself and onto Capitol Hill in this fashion. Nor did he admit that he and the Democratic leaders welcomed the opportunity to create a friendly, controlled environment in which suffrage advocates in the House could be sequestered and outside groups could air their grievances in a never-ending series of hearings, all without disrupting the House's work or committing the House to anything. Receiving credit from NAWSA for this was the cherry on top.

Elizabeth Bass regarded it as her responsibility to urge the president to do more for women. After working on Wilson's reelection campaign, she returned to Washington in March to start a Women's Bureau at the Democratic National Committee, where she was promoted based on her success in coordinating campaign activities in the twelve states where women voted. Her viewpoint was that of a working woman who began her career as a court reporter, married a former Republican state senator who was now an Illinois judge, and became a devout suffragist in the process. As an Illinois resident, she was entitled to vote for Wilson in the previous presidential election. She now believed Wilson was not doing enough to dispel the perception that he was uninterested in women's voting rights.

With the silent sentinels frequently voicing their concerns before the White House in the May sunshine, Bass gently urged the president to grant "a five-minute interview" to four of the country's leading women: Jane Addams, Lillian Wald, Florence Kelley, and Elizabeth Evans. She sold it as a method to highlight his commitments on social legislation that women care about, including improving labor standards, enforcing the first federal child labor law, and "preserving the social structure during the war." But Wilson recognized the names. True, they were all social reform leaders, but to women, they were suffragists.

George Creel set his machinery in motion at the Committee on Public Information headquarters, directly across the street from the White House, shortly after Wilson signed the Espionage Act on Friday, June 15.

The first steps were already taken. According to Creel's procedures, any branch of government affected by one of the CPI's stories was required to review and approve the material immediately. Today's piece about the Espionage Act had been distributed for approval earlier that day. It was then mass-produced using mimeographed stencils. As soon as the president signed the bill, Creel's team placed the tall stacks of paper in the pressroom for the news associations, newspapers, and radio stations with reporters stationed there 24 hours a day to collect official news.

The classifications were quite vague and unpredictable. A report regarding the movements of "alien labor," which refers to foreign-born U.S. laborers, was one example of restricted subject matter supplied by the restrictions. Creel asked editors to report even seemingly regular content to the CPI if they had any doubts. This unprecedented regime of federal press surveillance, which he called "self-censorship" but was actually direct regulation, now has significant support in the guise of the Espionage Act's harsh penalties.

To make compliance easier, the Creel Committee established itself as a source of all news for the press. It promptly hired an army of journalists who, in addition to reporting from headquarters, were embedded in various government agencies, including the Departments of Justice, War, Navy, and Labor. Liaisons were swiftly established at the Departments of State and Treasury, and the list grew to encompass nearly the entire US government. departed from "the peacetime practice of the press with its uninterrupted daily swing of reporters through the various departments, the buttonholing of clerks, and the haphazard business of permitting minor officials to make unchecked and unauthorized statements," Creel lamented.

The CPI's Division of News became journalism's primary point of contact, deciding what information was appropriate for publication and delivering it in a simple pre-written newspaper format. At its discretion, the committee may grant a reporter's request for an interview with a government official, but in each case, it will insist on making the preparations itself.

Except for Sundays, the Creel Committee published a model newspaper for the national press to follow. It was known as the Official Bulletin, and its emblem was the Great Seal of the United States. The content was organized in newspaper columns, with proposed headlines atop each article.

Each edition of the Official Bulletin contained a substantial amount of material, often lasting nearly fifty pages, allowing a conforming publisher to simply copy the contents at a large savings while simultaneously avoiding legal culpability. The committee's objective was to fill the hole left by censorship by flooding the information channels with government-produced news. Working round the clock, CPI produced around six thousand newspaper columns per week. It also produced a weekly digest in galley form, allowing a newspaper on a small budget without Washington reporters or a wire service to cut costs.

Both men agreed the word "censorship" should be avoided. The CPI's pro-administration advertising was to be dubbed "an information service," as Wilson designated it in his executive order. The sheer volume of material generated by the CPI would draw attention away from the committee's censorship actions. "The suppressive features of the work must be so overlaid by the publicity policy that they will go unregarded and unresented," Creel stated in his original plan, which Wilson approved.

In the view of the Committee on Public Information, each additional visit to the White House by a wartime ally provided more evidence that the suffrage protests on Pennsylvania Avenue were antiwar action. Every general, ambassador, and head of state who entered the White House had to go through the picket lines of the silent sentinels. Every one of them was met with harsh condemnation of America's commander in chief, boldly splashed onto the banners carried by the mute women.

The tipping moment occurred in the summer of 1917, when Wilson appointed Nobel Peace Prize laureate and former Secretary of State Elihu Root as "Ambassador Extraordinary" to head a diplomatic mission to Russia. Wilson's goal was to persuade the young Russian republic to rejoin the war against Germany. This would benefit the Allies by requiring Germany to keep significant forces committed to the Eastern Front. Root was a staunch opponent of women's suffrage, but to achieve the mission's goal, he sought favor with the new Russian administration, exaggerating the similarities between the world's oldest and newest democracies. He stressed that women have the right to vote in both America and Russia.

Unaware of the backlash Wilson would face at home, the Creel Committee arranged for one million copies of Root's talk to be printed and distributed in both Russia and the United States. Alice Paul, Lucy Burns, and the National Woman's Party leaders did not have to wait for an official copy because the misleading passage was quoted in the New York Times just a few days later. Their reactions were predictable. They held Wilson accountable.

On June 20, as British suffragist Emmeline Pankhurst met with Root in Petrograd, Paul and Burns meticulously crafted a factual response to the administration's assertion. "President Wilson and Envoy Root are deceiving Russia," they claimed, since "twenty million American women are denied the right to vote." That, of course, was correct. NAWSA president Carrie Chapman Catt also chastised Root for falsely claiming "the 'universality' of a suffrage which excluded half the people," and published her criticism in NAWSA's magazine, the Woman Citizen.Wilson.

As the gathering quickly turned into a mob, the two women froze in their seats, terrified for their safety and clutching the flag as hard as they could. They said nothing, just as they always did. Their cheeks became pale as the mob pushed toward them, forcing them up against the White House fence. Despite the violent assault on the women, White House security and D.C. police did nothing to protect them, disperse the mob, or apprehend the thugs. Instead, they took quiet notes, copying down the silent sentinels' potentially "treasonous" message.

A man punched his fist through the flag. Then others joined in the assault, yanking the banner from the women's grasp and tearing it apart. Nonetheless, the White House and D.C. police did little to stop the marauders. Concerned exclusively with Burns and Lewis' anti-Wilson message, federal investigators rushed to retrieve the shredded banner to serve as "evidence."

The administration acted quickly, considering alternatives such as declaring a military zone around the White House and closing the National Woman's Party offices. Pullman addressed the assembled journalists after his meeting with Tumulty. He clarified that the White House was in command of police picketing policy. Specifically, arrests would be performed solely on direct orders from the White House. When "White House officials request that the police department change its policy," it will comply.

According to press reports, Wilson was already sending commands previous to this. Nonetheless, "President Wilson would not say the word to cause the desired arrest."

Pullman's next move suggested Wilson had determined it was the moment. Immediately after leaving the White House, the police chief informed the quiet sentinels that it would be "unwise" for them to picket again, and if they did, they would face arrest.

Creel's wartime censorship, backed up by the prospect of criminal punishment, had a significant impact on newspaper coverage of the day's protests. The Russian banner episode occurred only six days after Wilson signed the Espionage Act, which imposed strong criminal penalties for any remarks the administration deemed to "obstruct" the war effort. The Espionage Act gave Postmaster General Albert Burleson—a former Democratic congressman and Wilson's loyal ally who had been the first to push Jim Crow across the federal government—unrestricted authority to determine what statements could be considered obstructive. If he determined that a newspaper or magazine held opinions adverse to Wilson's war policy, he might remove it from the mails without court sanction. Violations of this section of the law were also punishable by five years in prison.

As a result, publishers were intimately aware of what Wilson intended them to print. Not only were papers loyal to Wilson, such as the New York Times, but traditionally Republican-leaning papers, such as the New York Tribune and Chicago Tribune, ran with the administration's narrative that the suffragists picketing the White House, rather than their violent attackers, were to blame and should be arrested. Protesters were, per Burleson's directive, seeking to "embarrass" the president.

The general opinion was succinctly described in a weekend editorial following the banner incidents, titled "Shut Up or Be Locked Up!" Without any irony, the editors of the Chicago Day Book began by declaring their unwavering confidence in free speech. "But that was during peacetime. "Now we're at war," they clarified. Citizens should no longer be allowed to "freely rail against the government." Those who do, especially from "the steps of official buildings," should be "incarcerated. "They belong there, and now is the time to lock them up."

Despite the tightening noose of negative press coverage, the silent sentinels remained unconcerned, confident that they had achieved their goal of keeping women's voting rights on page one, even during warfare. The newspapers, while hostile, recognized the demonstrators' strategic accomplishment. Their "offensive" banners may have been ripped to shreds, according to the Washington Post, "but the suffragists succeeded in getting the thing they were after—advertising."

Chapter 12: 'Traitor'

THE PRESIDENT'S GOOD FRIEND AND POLITICAL REPRESENTATIVE IN NEW YORK CITY was taking chances with his career. Dudley Field Malone made news the day before the Bastille Day demonstration when he spoke at an emergency meeting of the American Union Against Militarism (later the American Civil Liberties Union) to denounce Postmaster General Burleson's censorship under the Espionage Act.

After attending the Bastille Day vigil to witness the police treatment of the silent sentinels and to advise the women of their rights, Malone hastened to the office of D.C. commissioner Louis Brownlow to complain. Brownlow, like his police chief Pullman, feared that the disloyal suffrage pickets were under German control and gave no consolation. Malone browbeat Brownlow with "a protest loud and long," during which he introduced Doris Stevens as a "friend" of his.

Attorney General Thomas Gregory also observed Malone's attendance at the Bastille Day gathering, which he discussed with him in person the next day. Gregory observed Malone and Stevens in the dining room at Chevy Chase Country Club. Gregory made it obvious to Malone that he did not support the suffrage protests while Stevens was present. The attorney general had been a key force behind the Espionage Act and was already planning a further increase of government power to silence dissent. It would become legislation in a few months under the name Sedition Act.

The judge relented the next day. He dismissed Malone's testimony, and Stevens' closing argument that the women's peaceful demonstration was protected under the First Amendment. Taking a dubious view of the idea that putting up a flag was "speech," he railed against the weeks-old Russia sign, calling it "treasonable and seditious." It was a surprising statement from the bench in a court of law, where treason is defined as an attempt to subvert the government and is punishable by death—especially given that the Russia sign was not even in question in this case.

What may explain such a disproportionate sentence for the offense? The Board of Commissioners, ever sensitive to the president's intentions, wanted the anti-Wilson rallies to end. The District's corporation counsel, who reported to them, urged Judge Mullowney to impose the maximum penalty. The judge, who had worked as a city prosecutor for many years before Roosevelt chose him to the bench, sympathized with them. He frequently socialized with the District's prosecution team, even sharing a box with one of them at Washington Nationals baseball games. His impolitic remarks from the bench demonstrated that he supported their goal of terminating the protests. The punishment was not intended to suit the "crime," but rather to keep the suffragists away from Washington, where they could no longer humiliate Wilson. The women were sentenced to hard labor in rural Virginia, far from the capitol and the Washington press corps.

The sixteen inmates, like their fellow suffragists before them, refused to pay their fines. Within hours, they had melded into a faceless mass of offenders jammed into a train bound for the Occoquan prison workhouse.

Wilson's frustration with shutting down antiwar newspapers was unsurprising. He was adamant about penalizing dissent, but he didn't enjoy dealing with the political ramifications. With next year's midterm elections approaching, he couldn't afford to lose his congressional majority. It was consequently critical for him to reach an agreement with the coalition's left flank. On this day, he had to compensate for his postmaster general's lack of bedside manner. George Creel might at least pretend to agree with the civil libertarians, but Burleson was typically blunt. He utilized a boilerplate letter to respond to complaints of his strident censorship, even sending it to disgruntled members of Congress. The letter claimed that answering their questions would be "incompatible with the public interest."

Today, Wilson was sending a response to another member of the organization, Amos Pinchot, in an attempt to quell the mutiny among former allies. Wilson had previously expressed to Pinchot "a great deal of interest and sympathy" for the ADAM's complaints about Post Office censorship and promised to discuss the issue with Burleson "to see just how the case may best and most justly be handled." While Wilson was unwilling to make a public statement in favor of their viewpoint, as requested by the group, he believed that a personal response would help to heal the wound. "These are very sincere men," he urged Burleson, "and I should like to please them."

Burleson took his cue and wrote a letter that sounded so similar to Woodrow Wilson that the president transmitted it to Pinchot as his response, thus adopting it as his own. The Post Office Department has no intention of suppressing free criticism of the government, right or wrong. The government has promised not to interfere with legitimate expression of views regarding the war with Germany or any other matter. This was worthless double language, because Wilson and Burleson continued to enforce the Espionage Act and even prosecuted their court action against Eastman's publishing on this very issue. However, Wilson handled such controversies in his own way. He thought his calming comments would temper the group's public criticism.

Dudley Malone, who had just openly sided with the AIM and their concerns, selected this opportunity to storm into Wilson's office. According to the press, he approached the White House meeting shivering with "nervous energy," his voice "trembling" with "resentment over the attitude of the National Administration." He was there to protest not censorship, but the sentencing of suffragists and Wilson's refusal to endorse the Anthony Amendment. Because he had no appointment, Tumulty could only give him a brief meeting with the president. The extraordinary meeting, however, would last forty-five minutes.

Using his years of intimate working relationship with Wilson, Malone launched an outraged condemnation of the arrests, the District government's decision to prosecute, and the judge's outrageously harsh sentencing for a petty infraction. Above all, he was upset with the president for failing to act in support of the Anthony Amendment. For any White House, it was an unprecedented encounter.

Wilson said nothing except that he wanted to know more. He asked Malone for the complete story on why he was so concerned, and he invited him to express his personal thoughts about the situation.

Malone went on to tell Wilson everything he had seen during the Bastille Day rally, from the time the suffragists were detained in front of the White House to their sentencing in court that afternoon. He emphasized that, while one may not agree with the "manners" of women holding up political flags, all citizens have the right to petition the president or any other government figure for redress of grievances.

Wilson noted that the women had been unmolested at the White House gates for over five months. He carefully chose his words to demonstrate empathy without making a commitment.

Malone was getting closer to directly accusing the president. His sources for this information, he claimed, were "newspapermen of unquestioned information and integrity." They informed him that the District government's "carefully laid plans" for the arrests and trials of the suffragists were developed in collaboration with Joe Tumulty and Treasury Secretary McAdoo. According to the reporters, McAdoo, Wilson's son-in-law, played a direct role in deciding the arrest policy.

The indictment of Wilson's direct subordinates, which implied presidential culpability, put him on the defensive. The president retorted vehemently that he was not responsible and denied knowing anything about what the others were doing.

Malone cited his prior recommendation that the president declare women's suffrage "an urgent war measure and a necessary part of America's program for world democracy." Wilson had not done it. Malone pushed him again.

The president rejected the notion.

Malone noted the president was visibly moved by these final statements. They had actually had a long and close connection. In a letter to Malone last summer, the president expressed his admiration for her actions and his trust in her. I truly hope I will always deserve it.

If any such ideas crossed Wilson's mind, the daydream came to an abrupt end with Malone's next words.

"I cannot and will not remain in office and see women thrown into jail because they demand their political freedom."

When confronted with the threat that Malone's noisy exit over the suffrage issue would pose in today's political context, Wilson had to act immediately. He had already spent the day putting out fires on the left, so he could readily anticipate the headlines that Malone's resignation would bring. This, in turn, would elicit predictable responses from suffrage proponents throughout the political spectrum. For more than two years, the White House had received letters and telegrams from Democrats, Republicans, and practically every fraternal and benevolent organization in the country imploring the president to support the Anthony Amendment. This would simply increase the agitation.

Wilson's subsequent statements indicated he was determined to persuade Malone not to retire, at least not now. However, the attempt was sloppy, expressing his incredulity that Malone thought women's suffrage was so vital.

"What will the people of the country think when they hear that the Collector of the Port of New York has resigned because of an injustice done to a group of suffragists by the police officials of the city of Washington?" Wilson inquired.

"With all respect for you, Mr. President, my explanation to the public will not be as difficult as yours, if I am compelled to remind the public that you have been appointed to office and can remove all the important officials of the city of Washington."

Again, they were at odds. Wilson instantly softens his tone.

"I do not question your strong conviction on this issue," the president said kindly. "I know you've always been a staunch suffragist. And since you believe as you do, I see no reason why you should not become their attorney and appeal this case without resigning from my administration."

It was a significant advance in his efforts to prevent Malone from quitting. However, he had failed to make any concessions on the Anthony Amendment, which Malone saw as the entire objective of his visit.

The president had 24 hours to stop Malone from resigning. If he fails to do so, he will face further negative publicity.

Wilson called Louis Brownlow, interim president of the District of Columbia Board of Commissioners. Wilson informed Brownlow, "We had made a fearful blunder...we never ought to have indulged these women in their desire for arrest and martyrdom." Wilson was furious, Brownlow recalled later.

Brownlow's meetings with Wilson about the first Occoquan detainees occurred at a time when the presidency of the Board of Commissioners, Washington's equivalent of mayor, was about to fall vacant. Brownlow had been acting president while the incumbent, fellow journalist Oliver Newman, was on leave to train as an army officer. According to Washington publications, Wilson may shortly choose Newman's replacement.

Brownlow had been enjoying Tumulty's ability to route his calls directly to the president for the past month. He enjoyed the grandeur of standing alongside Wilson at public gatherings. Just two days after the Fourth of July arrests, Brownlow and the president stood side by side on the Ellipse as thousands of Home Defense League demonstrators passed in front of them.

The former journalist had already built a career of complimenting Wilson in his editorials and news reports, which is how he acquired the job as a commissioner in the first place. With the board presidency on the line, he promised Wilson that he was willing to accept full responsibility for all arrests and would alert the president in advance, which was exactly what Wilson wanted to hear.

Malone departed Shoreham early that morning, fresh from his altercation with Wilson, to see his clients in Occoquan. He started the 25-mile drive, largely on dirt roads with speed limits of 15 and 20 miles per hour, early enough to arrive at his destination by ten o'clock. He then rushed back to Washington in the late afternoon for a clandestine meeting with the appellate counsel he had hired to fight the government's actions.

As the two lawyers spoke discreetly in the Shoreham lobby, George

Creel approached them unexpectedly. A New York Times reporter documented the event. Creel declined to comment on how he got there or what happened between him and Malone. "It was said," the Times explained passively, that Creel "just happened to be present."

Hopkins began by recounting what he had seen in court the previous day. He described the proceedings as "outrageous and farcical." He urged Wilson to forgive all convicts soon. But he swiftly moved on from the maltreatment of suffrage demonstrators, on which he admitted he was biased, to Wilson's unwillingness to support the Anthony Amendment. This, he argued, was the source of the problem.

The "women of the country were aroused," Hopkins told the president, and the agitation against his presidency would continue "unless the Anthony Amendment was passed." Hopkins believed it was an issue of justice, and presidential leadership on the amendment was "the only solution."

Hopkins then revealed that he had already started polling Congress about the Anthony Amendment and had "proceeded far enough with the poll to justify the prediction that it will show more than a majority for it in the House and the necessary two-thirds vote in the Senate." Wilson urged him to finish the assignment and report back to him with the results. Hopkins agreed to do so "within a day or two."

Chapter 13: Terror

FOUR HOURS LATER, SEVERAL BEWILDERED police officers in the street outside the District Jail discovered that the ladies crammed into their two police vans would not be admitted to the jail under any circumstances. The jailers had orders to send the women to Occoquan.

The women in the police wagons strained to hear what was being said, but the vehicles had no windows or openings for sound to enter, except for a small vent on the roof. They only understood what was said when they resumed their movement. The vans were turning away from the jail!

The Occoquan veterans quickly knew they were about to board a train bound for the prison workhouse. They recalled this section of the long, ominous ride south down the western side of the Potomac. Dorothy Day listened as they shared their experiences of "what the prisoners had suffered at the hands of the violent keeper there, a man named Whittaker." Day observed that whether veterans or first-timers, they were now "all afraid."

Why were the women rerouted? Louis Zinkhan, the administrator of the District Jail, had recently been sanctioned by the Supreme Court of the District of Columbia for transporting a prisoner from his facility to Occoquan in defiance of the sentencing judge's order. He would not have wanted to be found accountable for doing so just a few weeks later. But in the previous case, he had followed the District commissioners' directives, and the same was likely true now.

From Whittaker's perspective, the night was just beginning. Each of the women would now receive a personal welcome to "hell let loose," as one of the convicts put it. Dora Lewis was tossed into her unlit stone cell "like a sack," smashed her skull against an iron bed, and passed out. Her cellmates Nolan and Alice Cosu cried over her corpse as she lay still on the floor, believing she had died.

The uproar drew Whittaker to the cell door. He barks out a command. "If you dare to speak, I'll put the brace and bit in your mouths and the straitjacket on your bodies."

"We were so afraid we kept absolutely motionless," Nolan remembered later, "but Mrs. Cosu was quite ill... She suffered a terrible heart attack and started vomiting. We called repeatedly... A cold wind rushed in from the outside, and we lay there shivering and hardly conscious till daybreak."

Across the corridor, where three men had thrown Lucy Burns into a cell after twisting her arms behind her back and "shaking her violently," she gathered herself and began calling out the names of her fellow captives to see who was present. Guards instructed her to stop. When she refused, they shackled her hands over her head and secured them to the bars of the jail door. Whittaker then appeared, red-faced, yelling, and threatening to bind her in a straitjacket and gag. The guards uncuffed her from the jail door sometime before dawn, but she remained handcuffed until sunrise. The cells were designed for a single prisoner and only had one bed, yet each cell housed three women. The jailers had tossed the single mattress on the floor to create a second bed, placing a thin straw mat on the small bed frame. When Burns was finally able to move, she sank on the floor beside Day.

It was bitterly cold. Few of the ladies slept because they were battered and bruised, in pain, and afraid of what would happen next. One was led away to the men's section, where she was told she would be "alone with the men," who "could do whatever they pleased with her."

It had not been 24 hours. The punishment, mental and physical, was just beginning. The jailers were well aware that keeping the situation out of the public eye would be critical. To that goal, a contingent of U.S. Marines were summoned in the middle of the first night from Quantico, Virginia, which is fifteen miles distant. Their role was to guard the prison, keeping curious minds out and irregular processes inside. In the coming days, Marine guards would turn away the women's family members and legal counsel.

As the days of their dismal November passed slowly, Alice Paul and Rose Winslow continued to suffer repeated force-feedings each day in the District Jail hospital. Three of their fellow demonstrators remained in solitary confinement in the jail's cramped quarters. Dora Lewis, Lucy Burns, and Philadelphia educator Elizabeth McShane had joined them in Occoquan in their own nightmare of forced feeding. Whittaker chose Lewis and Burns as the leaders of the sixteen convicts who remained on hunger strike, making them the first two to get the brutal punishment. McShane was discovered asleep on the floor of her cell after eight days of starvation, making her the third prisoner to be force-fed.

The Occoquan workers lacked procedural skills. McShane's stomach and gallbladder were damaged due to the tube being jammed down her throat. When District Jail physician James Gannon and a specialist examined Occoquan, they identified her ailments and proposed a regimen of "a reduced quantity of food" that would be force-fed more "slowly." However, doctors left and the practice remained unchanged.

The rest of the world was unaware of this great self-sacrifice. Thanks to the Marine guards' efficiency in keeping all would-be visitors away, including the prisoners' legal counsel, no newspaper was enticed to disobey George Creel's ban on reporting spectacular stories about suffragists in prison. However, one of the Marines, who had heard during his guard job that "unknown tortures were going on" within the prison, decided to drive all the way to Washington to notify the women at NWP headquarters. Armed with this information, Malone's co-counsel, Matthew O'Brien, who had been denied admittance to Occoquan twice before, promptly obtained an order from Judge Mullowney providing him immediate access to his clients.

He promptly returned to the jail workhouse, where waving the court order resulted in his entrance. O'Brien was startled by what he saw once inside. Whittaker's technique of mental torture and physical assault on Lucy Burns included stripping her of her prison garb, leaving her naked except for the blankets in her cell. That is how O'Brien discovered her, wrapped only in blankets and lying on a cot. He retrieved from her the tiny scraps of paper on which she had surreptitiously written each day's extraordinary happenings. After consulting with Burns, Dora Lewis, and Eunice Brannan, O'Brien realized he had more than enough evidence to support a petition for a writ of habeas corpus, which allows convicts to dispute the way their sentences are carried out. If successful, Whittaker would be forced to bring all the inmates to the courtroom, where a judge could view firsthand their appalling conditions.

The detective accompanied O'Brien throughout the round trip. Immediately after his return to Washington, an administration emissary arrived at Occoquan to persuade the women to withdraw their petition. He gave "a positive guarantee from the District Commissioners" that the women would be moved to the District Jail within a week if they agreed. The motivations were obvious: an open court hearing on the prison abuse of demonstrators protesting President Wilson was likely to make headlines. That was precisely what the White House did not want. The women declined the offer.

President Theodore Roosevelt appointed Edmund Waddill, a former United States attorney and Republican member of Congress, to the federal bench. The hearing was scheduled for November 23, a few days before Thanksgiving.

Two days before the hearing, Wilson read a letter from Vira Boarman Whitehouse, who had recently won a groundbreaking suffrage referendum in New York. She pronounced herself "distressed" at the force-feeding of Alice Paul and Rose Winslow in the District Jail, and the "tales about prison conditions at Occoquan." It was "painful to stand by and watch" as they underwent "excessive terms, as appears from the daily papers."

Tumulty delicately told Wilson that "the time is soon coming when we will have to seriously consider this matter." However, Wilson concluded that now was not the time. He instructed Tumulty to inform Whitehouse that "no real harshness of method is being used," and that the prisoners were "submitting to the artificial feeding without resistance." He also wanted Tumulty to explain that jail conditions "are being thoroughly investigated for the second or third time." As for the possibility of any abuses, Wilson directed him to state that "none has as yet been disclosed."

"They offended against an ordinance of the District," Wilson argued, "and are undergoing the punishment appropriate in the circumstances." Overall, Tumulty should make plain that there was "an extraordinary amount of lying about the thing."

The following day, Judge Waddill gazed in horror as the haggard, haunted-looking suffragist convicts dragged themselves into his courtroom. Some were unable to walk and relied on other convicts as human crutches. After a heroic effort to reach their chairs, the women sank half-prone onto them, battling to remain awake. One of them, Eunice Brannan, did not make it very far before collapsing on the floor and having to be helped out.

Malone and O'Brien were present as lawyers for the convicts. The government's witnesses included Occoquan Superintendent Whittaker, District Jail Superintendent Zinkhan, and the District's Corporation Counsel. Newspaper reporters occupied whatever space was left in the small courtroom. Counting heads, the majority but not all of the convicts were present, including the sad woman who had just been executed.

It quickly became clear that the government wanted to avoid sending the two ladies to court. They vehemently opposed it, with Whittaker testifying that he feared for their health if they were relocated. Malone and O'Brien felt that the government was concerned about allowing the judge to view the bruises and injuries they had sustained while in prison. They knew from shreds of notes smuggled out of the District Jail that Burns and Lewis could make the trek to Alexandria.

A good lawyer never raises a question in open court unless he already knows the answer. Malone was aware that Lucy Burns had resisted her force-feedings by refusing to open her clenched mouth, earning the protestors the nickname "iron-jawed angels" from anti-suffrage Republican Joseph Walsh of Massachusetts during a House debate. The jail officers replied by pushing the tube up her nostril and into her stomach, resulting in profuse blood and excruciating pain. She fought it every step of the way. It was an incredible Saturday hearing. Normally, the court did not meet on weekends, but given the detainees' condition, the judge understood the matter could not wait. The fact that Burns and Lewis seemed bruised and gaunt in their prison clothing reinforced the judge's suspicion that the government was lying. The wordless testimony of the convicts' appearance and the thorough written testimony they supplied were powerful—"bloodcurdling," stated the court. In his response to the government, he stated that the written testimony was "shocking to man's ideas of humanity if it is true…and yet your answer denies all these facts which they submit."

Zinkhan said Brownlow directed him to bring convicts to Occoquan at a meeting attended by all three commissioners. He admitted the presence of a fourth person, but stated he couldn't recall who it was. Malone pressed him, confident it was McAdoo, as he had told Wilson.

Three women were freed on medical parole because "they were so near collapse from what they had undergone at Occoquan," according to the New York Times. The judge feared that "further confinement would result in their deaths." The other suffrage convicts were returned to Washington to spend the remainder of their sentences as originally imposed. They would join Alice Paul, Rose Winslow, and the other women still incarcerated at the District Jail.

Protests protesting the president's refusal to support the Anthony Amendment made headlines again. Aside from publicizing the government's legal defeat, newspapers across the country published many of the graphic details of the prison abuses, compelling Wilson to respond. The following day, the Washington Evening Star reported that President Wilson had granted permission for two doctors to make "an inspection of the District workhouse at Occoquan."

On November 25, the Pittsburgh Gazette Times reported on the horrifying torture of suffrage demonstrators at Occoquan, and the administration's defeat in court for illegally imprisoning them. This attention came on the heels of Shaw's three-day visit to Pittsburgh, during which she roundly attacked the suffrage protests. The news headlines spurred Wilson's old friend Lawrence Woods, a Pittsburgh resident and Princeton alumnus with whom the president frequently corresponded, to send a note to Joe Tumulty with a suggestion.

Woods revealed his attempt to "kill the story" concerning the abuse of suffragettes. He would hire "the newspaper fellows in Washington" to paint them as the "neurasthenic, overwrought women anxious to pose as martyrs" they truly were. When asked who may accomplish this, Woods responded he was "very sure Dave Lawrence would if he is still in Washington."

David Lawrence, however, remained in Washington. He was the New York Evening Post's Washington correspondent, a Princeton graduate, and one of Wilson's former classmates, well-known for his strong links to the government. He was already on the case, having long been the president's strong defender.

Earlier in the week, Wilson's connections gave him access to four suffragist prisoners who were not allowed visitors: Alice Paul, Lucy Burns, Rose Winslow, and Elizabeth McShane. He also spoke with Superintendent Zinkhan and other jail personnel, lending credibility to his feature story that ran on the front page of the New York Evening Post on November 27. Lawrence acknowledged that he was getting two different versions of the facts from the women and their jailers, but he nonetheless concluded that "most of what the militants say is purposely exaggerated." He dismissed the notion that psychiatrists had examined Paul, because the jailers flatly denied it. He acknowledged that the sidewalk obstruction legislation "had been stretched." But he saw no reason for concern because sending the pickets to jail was important to "protecting the president's life." The women "would be promptly released" provided they "agreed to stop picketing."

Lawrence discussed other issues that he did not write about during his four-hour jail interrogation. He informed Paul that "the president would not mention suffrage in his message at the opening of Congress, but would make it known to the leaders of Congress that he wanted it passed." He then asked her what she would do if only one house of Congress passed the Anthony Amendment before the election. If the administration were to "go to the country in the 1918 elections on that record," with the purpose "to pass it through the other house a year from now," would she then agree to stop picketing?"Paul said she would not.

The White House, the District Board of Commissioners, and the Creel Committee made no comment on Lawrence's high-profile narrative, which was clearly designed to combat a wave of negative media highlighting maltreatment of suffrage inmates. However, on the day it appeared in the New York Evening Post, Superintendent Zinkhan publicly requested that Judge Mullowney release all twenty-two hunger-striking detainees from Occoquan. The following day, Zinkhan requested that the remaining nine suffrage inmates be released from the District Jail. Mullowney quickly issued both instructions.

Part IV: Victory and Defeat

Chapter 14: Death Warrant

THE HOLIDAYS CAME FAST. The day after Christmas, the president issued a proclamation that had a significant influence on holiday travelers. "I, Woodrow Wilson," declared he would "take possession and assume control at 12 o'clock noon on the twenty-eighth day of December, 1917, of each and every system of transportation and the appurtenances thereof located wholly or in part within the boundaries of the continental United States."

At the same time, Wilson designated his son-in-law, Treasury Secretary William McAdoo, as the "Director General of Railroads." According to the Seattle Star, the Wilson administration will "henceforth practically control every industry and business," in addition to the existing "government control of food, fuel, and foreign commerce." In view of such weighty government responsibilities, the New York Times spoke out against "the noisy feminine demonstrations" for the Anthony Amendment and the "insistence upon this minor and negligible question at this of all times." The Times ridiculed the idea that "a national election in war is to be decided by tempestuous petticoats."

The same day's mail included a message from NAWSA's White House liaison Helen Gardener, who wondered if Tumulty had forgotten about her plea to involve the president "to secure the number of votes needed—and from Democrats." She was not giving up, saying, "Here is still hoping."

That death warrant would be endorsed by NAWSA itself, she stated, as part of its new campaign strategy against Anthony Amendment opponents. Gardener added that "this is not said in the spirit of a threat," but the necessity for a disclaimer implied otherwise. This organization would "naturally make its campaigns against men and not against parties—but" (and that's when the covert threat arrived) "unless the Democratic Party sees a great white light before January 10, it will hit a good deal harder in the ranks of Democracy than in those of Republicanism." She described it as "simply the reading of the inevitable."

Gardener went on to detail the results of NAWSA's recently conducted poll of House members, which indicated "absolutely" that if the Anthony Amendment is repealed, "it will be the Democratic Party who denies women [her] constitutional right." In addition, she said, NAWSA possessed "the data to prove that the defeat by the Democratic Party of the suffrage amendment at this session of the Congress will also be the sure defeat of the Democratic Party at the next presidential election and the loss of the control of the House before that time."

The revelation that NAWSA had conducted a new poll of the House would have piqued Wilson's curiosity, as despite his aspirations for a current whip count, the Democratic whip group had yet to survey its members. The prohibition amendment had passed the House just before the holidays (ironically, with an overwhelming support from states' rights members), allowing the whip team to focus on the Anthony Amendment in earnest. But Thomas Bell, the majority whip, was uninterested in assisting it.

Taylor had perfect timing. Since Friday, the president had been working with Colonel House on his speech outlining America's war goals, but by Monday afternoon, the text was ready for approval by Secretary Robert Lansing at the State Department, leaving Wilson to focus on other issues. Armed with this new intelligence from Capitol Hill showing that the Anthony Amendment could pass the House in less than 72 hours, Secretary of the Navy Josephus Daniels and Treasury Secretary McAdoo issued remarks the next day, after Wilson gave his approval. However, the president made no sign of support.

The next morning, two days before the vote, the president started his day like so many others: with a round of golf. Edith joined him on the round trip to and from the golf club, where she played alongside him. The two returned to the White House by ten thirty, when Wilson, indulging in his imperious view of the proper relationship between the president and Congress, directed his staff to notify Speaker Champ Clark and Senate majority leader Thomas Martin that he wished to address a joint session in less than two hours, at twelve thirty. There had been no previous notification to Capitol Hill or the Cabinet. It was the first time Tumulty heard.

The president cannot call a joint session of Congress. Instead, both chambers must pass a concurrent resolution. In response to Wilson's surprise request, the whips frantically placed hundreds of urgent phone calls, while couriers fanned out to senators and representatives, with the result that "members commandeered practically every taxicab in town" trying to make it to the Capitol for the vote. In record speed, both chambers of Congress passed the enabling resolution and convened in the House chamber shortly before the president arrived.

The possibility of these agreements coming to light had arisen the previous month, when Russia's brief democracy gave way to revolutionary anarchy. As the Bolsheviks took control of the country's capital, Petrograd, they soon acquired Russian government offices, gaining access to a plethora of documents detailing the specific secret agreements to which the now-deposed czarist dynasty had made Russia a party. By revealing each nation's plans for dividing up hoped-for territorial conquests in the event of an Allied triumph, the documents intended to make the Great War appear to the rest of the world as simply another in a long string of European power grabs.

The Wilson administration was aware of some of these secret agreements prior to entering the war. They became aware of another in May 1917, when the Bolshevik journal Pravda published an article by its editor and party leader, Vladimir Lenin, describing the provisions of the secret Treaty of London. That treaty promised Italy geographical gains as an incentive to join the war.

More recently, further secret deals involving Britain and France were revealed owing to an early Bolshevik version of Wikileaks. One week before Thanksgiving, Pravda published a bombshell: according to a document in the czar's files, Britain and France intended to split up the Middle East for themselves, replacing the Ottomans. Lenin referred to it as "an agreement of the colonial thieves." The official explanation of the accord, known as the Sykes-Picot Agreement after the British and French officers who negotiated it, was published in Pravda on November 23.

Wilson took his place at the rostrum in the House chamber while late-arriving lawmakers were still racing to their seats. He began by addressing the "Gentlemen of the Congress," ignoring Jeannette Rankin's attendance. He then read the 2,500 words from his prepared text. The first of his fourteen points, "Open covenants of peace, openly arrived at," effectively rejected the secret accords before they became generally known, gaining the rhetorical upper hand.

Wilson's message also aimed to inspire the Bolsheviks, with the expectation that Russia would stay an ally in the war. According to Oxford historian and journalist Godfrey Hodgson, Wilson was "under the delusion that the Bolsheviks were essentially liberal allies," notwithstanding Lenin's obstinate antagonism to both sides of the war. Even then, Russia's revolutionary instability appeared to be primed for authoritarianism. The Washington Post's front page read, "Tyranny and Crime Reign in Petrograd," the morning after Wilson's address. In less than eight weeks, Bolshevik Russia will reach a separate peace with Germany.

Other Fourteen Points speech themes, such as national self-determination, freedom of the seas, global free trade, abandonment of territorial ambitions, and fairness to the German people, would be either ignored or completely forgotten by the Allied powers. However, the fourteenth point, which Wilson referred to as a "association" of states, would withstand the Allies' quest for territorial gains and reparations at the peace table the following year. More than any other term on his list, it reflected Wilson's idealism. Aside from practical considerations, it was a message that Americans really needed to hear in the midst of such sacrifice.

Wilson exited the House chamber shortly following his remarks, declining to share pleasantries with members of Congress or the invited dignitaries. As he exited the Capitol grounds from the Senate side, riding behind Colonel House behind the chauffeur, he may have unintentionally crossed paths with Dudley Field Malone, who was entering the courthouse just across the street. Reporters were fortunate to discover a space that hung on every word.

Three judges peered down on Malone and O'Brien from behind an elevated mahogany bench flanked by two American flags. On the wall above, a carved gold eagle perched over the United States shield. The court clerk and marshal each had their own little workstations on either side of the bench. The counsel tables in front of the bench, where Malone and O'Brien would move when their case was called, sat empty.

When their case was called, Malone and O'Brien sat on the left side of the table, while Conrad Syme, the District's Corporation Counsel, and two of his assistants sat on the right. Francis Stevens, one of the assistant counsels, made the opening statement for the government. Soon, O'Brien would respond to the suffragists' argument. He and Malone had written a lengthy brief that was sent to the justices ahead of time, citing more than thirty precedents, including U.S. Supreme Court judgments. It maintained that the indictment for sidewalk obstruction did not describe what the suffragists did to violate the D.C. ordinance.

The judges began questioning Stevens before the government had finished its opening presentation. The elderly Wyoming judge questioned how a single-file line of women up against the White House fence at the sidewalk's border could "obstruct the sidewalk," given that "it is commonly known there is a forty-foot sidewalk there."

The clean-shaven judge from Vermont questioned why, if other individuals jammed the sidewalks or, worse, resorted to violence because they disagreed with the message on the banners, they should not be arrested instead of peaceful protestors. He presented Stevens with a hypothetical inquiry about Billy Sunday, the notoriously controversial baseball player turned evangelist.

When Wilson returned to his desk in the White House, old business awaited. Tumulty had left him a note again, asking if he would meet with Representative Taylor and a group of Democratic House members. The secretary had attempted to receive an answer the day before but had been unsuccessful. With barely two days until the vote on the Anthony Amendment, Congressmen were highly concerned that they had not heard from the President. They required the meeting, Tumulty added, "so that they could be assured that you were not opposed to the suffrage amendment."

It was a leap to compare Lincoln's years of battle against slavery to what Wilson may or might not do with a few words at the end of others' seventy-year struggle. But Bass knew from experience that an argument on the merits would be met with the standard response of states' rights, a desire not to offend legislators, and so on. For the same reason, she appealed to his partisanship. She said Republicans should not have "the advantage of our silence to carry into congressional campaigns next year." Regarding what Wilson's southern Democratic friends would think, she highlighted that "the most extreme advocates of state rights abandoned their position entirely and passed the Prohibition Amendment."

Wilson merely needed to "say that word," she urged. It may come out "today or tomorrow, said to a few Democratic Congressmen or printed in the public press." Bass had made things easy for him. But when today turned into tomorrow, the president still did not answer.

Tumulty arrived at work the next morning, boosted by overwhelmingly good news about Wilson's address. It was customary for the secretary to snip what was vital to Wilson, and it was enjoyable today. The outstanding coverage of yesterday's presentation described it as "momentous," "remarkable," "memorable," "heartening," and a dozen other wonderful things. He couldn't help but notice two more stories on the main page that day. One was that Billy Sunday, the renowned preacher who was currently in Washington to deliver the opening prayer in Congress, had given a powerful endorsement of women's suffrage. The other was that the Anthony Amendment would surely win the House vote tomorrow.

Wilson was undoubtedly focused on the Anthony Amendment that day, as evidenced by two letters he wrote on the subject. His messages were practically identical, replying to two urgent demands for his assistance. One was addressed to Elizabeth Bass during the Democratic National Convention. The other was sent to Jouett Shouse, a Democratic representative from Kansas. They both started with the following: "It is extremely hard to reply to generous letters like yours without seeming to do violence to my real personal sentiments." In the few enigmatic phrases that followed, Wilson gave no indication of what those personal feelings may be.

Wilson's letter stated that he only provided "advice to members of

Congress when they have asked for it," and that "when they do ask, you know what the advice is." Yet here was Shouse, a member of Congress requesting the president's response on the eve of the vote, and Wilson refused to take a firm opinion. If House was meant to "know," he would have had to rely on what he heard from his House colleagues who had recently talked with Wilson on the matter. The Arkansas congressional delegation, all Democrats who had committed support for the Anthony Amendment, met with Wilson soon before Christmas and left "without getting any encouragement with regard to the Federal Amendment," according to the New York Times.

Bass at the DNC could not obtain a straight answer from the president. Wilson's letter stated that "you may readily conjecture what the advice is," leaving her grabbing air like everyone else.This time, the secretary's urgings were successful. With mere hours until the vote, Tumulty scheduled the meeting for business to end that evening. On Capitol Hill, Colorado Representative Ed Taylor quickly rallied some of the most ardent Democratic supporters of the Anthony Amendment, and a few new converts, for an emergency trip to the White House.

Chapter 15: 'The Apex of My Glory'

By mid-afternoon On December 4, America faded from view for the passengers aboard the world's third-largest cruise ship. The First Couple spent their early hours on board the recently rechristened USS George Washington, the same luxury liner that had transported Wilson's daughter Jessie and her husband, Francis Sayre, on their honeymoon to Europe six years before. During the war, the ship was commandeered as a troop transport, carrying thousands of service personnel to and from Europe. Now it was the commander in chief's personal vehicle. Wilson described his ten-day, 3,300-mile journey to France as "one of the pleasantest voyages I have ever taken."

In the lap of such luxury, increasingly removed from Washington, Wilson might easily lose sight of America's domestic issues, even postponing real preparation for the treaty discussions, which would not begin for another six weeks. He took a three-hour snooze every day of the ten-day journey, which could sometimes last four hours. He'd "then sleep again at night undisturbed." According to the president's daily activity log, he often slept until eleven or noon. On the other side of the ship, So did Edith. "We had one or two guests to lunch or dine with us nearly every day," Edith told me. "Then there was shuffleboard on deck," and before dinner and a movie, the couple would wander the glass-enclosed promenade deck together. "Life was serene," she recalled warmly.

While the Fourteen Articles piqued the interest of newspaper readers back home, Wilson's access to information was almost cut off. Radio communication using Morse code was time-consuming, and the crew frequently used the wireless telegraphy equipment for navigation and weather updates. He was left with only the ship's daily news report and Tumulty's prioritization of the most essential letters. He quickly lost contact with the nation he led.

The day after the Fourteen Articles were published in full in Washington newspapers, the president spoke with Ray Fosdick, a former Princeton student who was lounging in one of the ship's conference rooms. Wilson had previously recruited him to the DNC's finance committee; now he was assigned to the peace conference as a

War Department official. "The President sat at the table and we swapped Negro stories," Fosdick wrote in his diary, with Wilson's stories "easily out-rivaling mine." The president "had just started to tell of a darky's comment," wrote Fosdick, as Edith entered the room, looking to take her husband "for a walk around the decks." But instead of interfering, Fosdick remembered, she participated in the fun and "told us to go to it."

Wilson, however, refused to authorize Tumulty to send a note to Gay, Shields, or Pollock. He had reasons. Despite Tumulty's confidence in Shields, the Tennessean sent Wilson a polite but firm letter six months ago stating that the Anthony Amendment offended his "most profound convictions." Pollock, too, seems to have made up his mind—to vote "yes." In October, South Carolina's governor, Richard Manning, wrote to Wilson that he believed Pollock was "disposed to vote" for the amendment. But he had suggested Wilson invite the newly appointed Pollock to the White House for a reassuring conversation. Wilson had not done so while still in Washington, preferring to avoid such contacts, and it was now impossible as he traveled to France.

Robert Ewing was an unlikely pick for the position. For twenty-five years, as the proprietor of many Louisiana newspapers, including the New Orleans States and the Shreveport Times, he had been railing against Anthony. Wilson knew Ewing well; as the New York Times put it, the two men were "intimate friends." Their friendship began in 1912, when Ewing, as Louisiana's Democratic national committeeman, played a key role in securing Wilson's Democratic presidential candidacy. He then worked as national co-manager on Wilson's two presidential campaigns. He is still a DNC member and has had a significant impact on southern Democratic politics.

Gordon proposed a Louisiana state constitutional amendment in 1907 to extend voting privileges to the "white female" population. Her thinking has become more polished over the last decade. Now she fantasized about rephrasing the Anthony Amendment in more delicate language that would achieve the same result, avoiding the trap that John Sharp Williams had so well demonstrated with his futile efforts to insert the words "white women" into the Constitution. In a letter to a fellow southern suffragist shortly after the Louisiana amendment was defeated, she described how her method would work.

Her initial thinking was to collaborate with Senator Charles S. Thomas of Colorado, the Senate Committee on Woman Suffrage's immediate previous chairman. However, she quickly moved her focus to her own newly elected senator, Edward Gay, in part because NAWSA headquarters in New York had been pressuring her to secure Gay's vote since the November election.

Despite her retirement as a NAWSA executive, Kate Gordon remained a member, as did her sister, Jean, president of the New Orleans-based Louisiana Woman Suffrage Association. Their state organization was a NAWSA associate and had a positive working relationship with NAWSA's leadership. During the recent referendum on Louisiana's state suffrage amendment, the New York headquarters followed Kate Gordon's advice to remain out of the fight, citing Ewing's desire that they "leave the Federal Amendment question entirely out of the campaign." NAWSA's Ida Husted Harper faithfully reported to Gordon shortly after the election, "I was careful not even to write a letter to one of your newspapers during your campaign."

Harper now requested a favor in exchange for his help. "Your Senator Gay could and possibly would give the lacking vote," she wrote Gordon on November 18, cautiously adding, "if your organization would consent."

Harper informed Gordon that "new Senator Pollock of South Carolina has pledged his vote in favor," emphasizing why only one more vote was required—and Gay should be their primary target. Gordon recognized that she, Ewing, and their allies would need to work quickly. Another Republican might step forward at any time to push the Anthony Amendment over the top, giving them little leverage to change its text. She was therefore much relieved to learn from Harper that NAWSA was "extremely anxious that the other vote also shall be Democratic in order that the Republicans cannot claim a partisan advantage." NAWSA would consequently stop recruiting Republicans. This was at Wilson's request. "President Wilson saw at what disadvantage the party would be placed at the next election," explains Harper, "and that was the reason why he endeavored to save the situation."

Creel had always wanted Wilson "to go to Paris in person, to sit at the Peace Table himself." He imagined Wilson on the world stage, where he would "stand out as America's source of power, America's chosen champion," with CPI cameras and journalists filming his every action for reply back home. David Lawrence accused Creel for promoting Wilson's trip on the advice of the president's friends, who found it even more difficult "to understand why George Creel should be taken to Europe." Because there was no peace conference and no firm date for its start, Wilson and Creel, joined by Colonel House, devised a schedule of luncheons, gala receptions, and outdoor events such as parades and military honors, all of which would result in the stunning visual displays Creel envisioned. While still at sea, he planned Wilson's visits to "England, France, Italy, and possibly Germany." There was now enough time for these trips.

On December 16, while the president was touring the palace at Versailles with Edith and making plans to play golf, William Monroe Trotter arrived in Washington, D.C. from Boston to open a convention at which hundreds of Black men and women representing 37 states drafted an appeal to Wilson and the peace delegates in Paris. Trotter slammed America's "utterly undemocratic treatment of colored people" during his speech to the National African Congress for World Democracy. If the president had abandoned these issues by traveling to Europe, American supporters of genuine democracy would have crossed the ocean to find him. The convention chose eleven "peace delegates" to travel to France and demand that "full democracy for colored Americans be made a part of the world's peace settlement."

Even after the war ended, the administration used this broad authority to establish a blanket prohibition on Black Americans' travel. In pursuance of this policy, the State Department denied passports to all but a few Black applicants. National Woman's Party members were similarly targeted, as two NWP ladies learned when attempting to board a ship bound for Paris. An American officer at the port of embarkation abruptly invalidated their previously issued passports, which had recently been stamped with British and French visas. "the State Department has ordered me to take your passports away," the official informed them, refusing to explain the situation further. Eventually, the State Department issued a statement explaining why the passports were recalled. It was, the government maintained, "because the President would be greatly embarrassed if they were in Paris at the same time he was there."

Trotter and his colleagues, unable to leave the nation, continued with their convention for global democracy in Washington, while the NWP continued with their inventive attempts to win Wilson's attention from a distance. On December 16, the day after the president laid a wreath at Lafayette's tomb in Paris, members of the Woman's Party held their own ceremonial event in the United States capital. More than 300 banner-bearing ladies went by the vacant White House in silence. The torchbearer at the head of the procession then started a fire at the base of Lafayette's statue. Women once again set fire to Wilson's comments.

This manifestation of unhappiness stemmed from "thoughtful courage," according to Olympia Brown, 83, one of the oldest ladies who took part. She explained that the older participants linked today's youth to their forefathers, who "have fought for liberty for seventy years." They had all come, she explained, to "protest against the President's leaving America with this old fight here unwon." Elizabeth Selden Rogers, an Occoquan veteran who chaired the march, voiced the group's frustration. "While President Wilson has sailed away to Europe to obtain democracy for the world," she told me, "American women, after six years, know how hollow his words are."

As 1918 came to a close, it was uncertain when the peace conference would begin. Wilson's schedule of parties, award ceremonies, and parades, broken by infrequent meetings and speeches, remained on track, much to Creel's satisfaction. Following a round of Christmas shopping with Edith in Paris, the presidential entourage headed to England. Wilson's parade through London on December 26 was as grand as his reception in Paris. The route to his royal suite at Buckingham Palace was magnificently decorated with American flags, streamers, and Allied flags. His royal carriage and the sovereign's escort of Household Cavalry paraded past the massive crowds with the pomp of a coronation. At the palace, his personal servants, more than a dozen of them clad in white wigs, red coats, black velvet knee breeches, white silk stockings, and shoes with big silver buckles, responded to his every need. During his stay, the King's Guard and Welsh Guards stood vigil outside his door.

Hundreds of women suffragists continued to demonstrate for the Anthony Amendment in Lafayette Park, across the street from Tumulty's office, for a month after Wilson left. Time was running out for the lame-duck session of Congress, which began on December 2 and would end on March 4. Wilson still hadn't spoken with John Sharp Williams or any other senator regarding the Anthony amendment. By the time Tumulty dispatched his message from Washington, the president had traveled 300 miles from London to the small town of Carlisle, on the Scottish border, to visit the church built by his grandfather. It is unclear when he received the message; he did not answer until January 10. Even so, he ignored Tumulty's inquiry concerning Williams and instead asked ingeniously, "Is there anything else I can do to help bring about the passage of the Suffrage Amendment?"

January followed the same pattern as December, with the president using his free time for travel and ceremonies. Victor Fleming's team shot footage and stills of him in front of every major Roman tourist attraction as he strolled before colorful crowds in Italy. The president passed the Trevi Fountain, the Colosseum, the Spanish Steps, the Piazza della Repubblica, the Pantheon, and the Forum; he was at the Vatican with Pope Benedict XV, the Quirinal Palace with Prime Minister Vittorio Orlando, and Michelangelo's Campidoglio with King Victor Emmanuel.

But as the mayor of Rome, the king, and the prime minister draped even more medals over Wilson's shoulders, he realized that the official extravagance was due to the fact that Italy, like England and France, sought a share of the material gain from the peace treaty. And he, Woodrow Wilson, would have a significant vote in determining whether they would get it.

The peace conference, which had always been the focal purpose of Wilson's presence in Europe, eventually began on January 12, albeit informally. Wilson complained to Edith's social secretary that not only did some of the delegates arrive late, but "two-thirds of the time" was spent on discussion and formality, which reminded him of "an old ladies' tea party." It would be six more days until the meeting officially began. It took two days to choose French President Georges Clemenceau as chairman, despite the fact that almost everyone agreed. Even the list of nations participating at the summit remained unclear, with Russia and its warring divisions posing the most challenging dilemma.

It wasn't until January 25, at the second formal meeting, that Wilson was given permission to chair a working committee to explore his League of Nations plan. For the next few months, that would be his top priority. He refused to delegate the work, jealousy maintaining his complete control over the issue. Wilson barred Secretary of State Lansing from participating in the peace conference, despite the fact that he was a delegate. Lansing was so startled by the president's angry attitude that he pondered retiring. The secretary was left with no doubt that his counsel "was unwelcome," and that Wilson wished him to "keep away from the subject of the League."

By February 3, Wilson had made enough headway on his draft proposal for the League to present it to his committee members. However, because they did not all understand English, it took another day before translations of his written paper were completed. Before submitting the plan to the peace conference for debate, the committee had to reach an agreement among itself. However, there were significant conflicts; the French delegates were among the first to protest some aspects of the plan. Wilson's role of coordinating support was made more difficult when members from four new countries were added to his group.

The passage of time was becoming a severe issue. He still needed to leave for home on February 17 to get to Washington before the 65th Congress's third and final session ended on March 4. Even that would be pushing it, as travel time alone may cost him ten or more days, possibly longer if there is poor weather or other unanticipated obstacles at sea. Congress would not assemble again until the first Monday in December, one year after he departed Washington, unless he called a special session of the newly Republican-controlled House and Senate.

Chapter 16: Sex, Race, and Paris

THE HOUSE DOORKEEPER drew a deep breath before raising his voice to announce the approach of the next group of dignitaries. The House and Senate had convened once more for a combined session in the Capitol. The black-robed Supreme Court justices entered the House chamber first, followed by the beautifully uniformed Army, Navy, and Marine Corps leadership. Members of the president's cabinet, diplomats, and dignitaries, including former President William Howard Taft, occupied the front rows, while crowds packed the galleries.

The only person missing from this scene was Woodrow Wilson. However, a president continued to dominate the proceedings.

On this day, February 9, 1919, America's leaders were eulogizing Theodore Roosevelt, who had died abruptly from a heart attack one month before. Since then, Roosevelt has received extravagant public plaudits in the United States, rivaling Wilson's in Europe. Millions of people attended services in all cities. The New York Times said there had never been "national ceremonies in honor of the memory of any other public man in any country."

Nonetheless, Wilson's popularity, which had dipped following the November elections, had recovered considerably after the armistice and his triumphant European tour. Public criticism was now primarily directed at the Republican side of the aisle, though Democratic senators privately resented the president's departure with precedent in excluding them from the peace talks. But when it came to the Anthony Amendment, Wilson's newly polished image was inadequate to persuade another southern Democrat to support it. And the president denied contacting anyone.

After ignoring Tumulty's calls for over a month, Wilson finally wrote a brief message to John Sharp Williams. In 130 characters, he referred to his prior note to the senator, mailed shortly before he left America, which was so polite it bordered on apology. "If this is an outrageous or unjustified request," Wilson had gently conceded, "please rebuke me as you will." Williams took the given escape route and stood firm. When Josephus Daniels cabled Wilson that Florida Senator Park

Trammell was likely to come around with some presidential coaxing, the president responded with two brief phrases that contained no encouragement at all. Predictably, it fell short.

Tumulty also suggested the president write Delaware senator Josiah Wolcott, who was "on the fence" and needed "a little push." Wilson had already rejected Tumulty's previous request to do this, and he resisted again.

With so little time remaining to obtain the one vote, Tumulty felt it was critical that Wilson send another message to Williams as well. The senator's wife had stated that her husband was concerned about the approaching vote on the Anthony Amendment and wanted to satisfy the president. Tumulty sent Wilson two telegrams February 7, three days before the scheduled vote, emphasizing the significance of the opportunity. The president also did not answer those requests.

Wilson's final request from his White House secretary was to write North Carolina Senator Lee Overman. This is what the President did. His three-sentence wire began with a contrite "pardon me" for asking and concluded with the "fortunes of our party" as the sole explanation. Unsurprisingly, Overman found that argument unsatisfactory. Southern Democrats relied on Jim Crow laws to secure their party's fortunes. It was ludicrous to believe that granting Black women voting rights and explicitly permitting federal enforcement would improve their situation.

Jones was joined in making that point by newly elected South Carolina Senator Pollock, boosting hopes that he would follow through on his prior vow to support the Anthony Amendment. But Senator Hitchcock of Nebraska, whom Wilson had elected not to contact despite Tumulty's urgent plea, chose to oppose the amendment alongside the Democratic leader.

On the eve of the vote, the national press reported that the Anthony Amendment remained one vote short of the required two-thirds majority. The same newspapers stated that more than forty ladies were arrested on the walkway in front of the White House that day for burning a paper effigy of Woodrow Wilson. The arrests were made not just by District police but also by military police, an overreaction to a peaceful protest that occurred despite the military's lack of formal power to detain civilians. Although the conflict was done, the "stern hand of firm repression" continued to crush opposition. The women were now in custody, awaiting their hearings in Police Court.

With only hours until the vote, predicting the Anthony Amendment's chances was clear. Wilson had not been a factor. He had not converted any of the southern Democrats he met. Outside the South, all seven Democratic senators who voted "no" the last time—senators from the Northeast, Midwest, and West, including Nebraska's Hitchcock—appeared to be opposed again. Wilson had overlooked this group for personal reasons, preferring to engage with southern Democrats. Wilson did not contact any of the twelve Republicans who voted "no" in October, including those who had been among his staunchest allies throughout the conflict.

The hushed talk in the galleries came to a halt as Pollock organized his papers and prepared to speak. Senior members on the Senate floor examined their new colleague standing at his desk near the front. Pollock received the ideal spot on the floor from his deceased predecessor, "Pitchfork Ben" Tillman, who had served in the Senate for nearly a quarter century. At the start of the new Congress, another guy would claim that position based on seniority, and Pollock would be pushed to the back.

"Let this then be my excuse and apology," the South Carolinian started, "for the vote which I shall cast on the pending resolution."

He had not yet announced his vote. Suffragists of all types leaned forward in their seats to hear every word. There were no microphones.

"As a Senator coming from South Carolina," Pollock continued, "the State of John C. Calhoun, the leading exponent of State rights; the State that first exercised the right to secede from the Union," I affirm that "the Constitution of the United States was amended at Appomattox when Lee tendered his sword to Grant..." From that day onward, the most fundamental of all State rights was destroyed: the States' independent sovereignty ceased to exist."

This seemed to be an unequivocal rejection of the states' rights argument. However, as the sophisticated lawyer continued his statement, it became evident that he believed Robert E. Lee had not surrendered certain state prerogatives. Pollock then rivaled his predecessor, the late Pitchfork Ben, in racial rhetoric. In one breath, he praised the absent president for "speaking only as Woodrow Wilson can," and in the next, he explained why he agreed with Wilson. Even after the Anthony Amendment was added to the Constitution, Pollock wanted everyone to understand that only "white womanhood" would be permitted to vote in the South.

Pollock's lecture had taken a while. The Anthony Amendment was introduced unanimously in the Senate, disrupting all other essential end-of-session action that had previously been scheduled. After hearing every possible pro and con suffrage argument in prior discussions, almost everyone was waiting for the roll call. But two more senators insisted on speaking, exacerbating the anxiousness of the suffragists in the visitors' galleries, the men in the press gallery, and the rest of the United States Senate, all of whom wanted to know if that one final vote would happen.

The first senator to stand between the restless chamber and the answer to that issue was a Republican from New Jersey who wanted to change either the nation's immigration laws affecting marriage and citizenship or the Anthony Amendment. He had attempted to advance his ideas in past debates but had been unsuccessful. His colleagues repeatedly informed him that the resolution on the floor was no longer up for amendment. He went on for quite some time, testing almost everyone's patience in the chamber.

The last man to ascend had a different narrative. There was enormous curiosity in hearing what Edward J. Gay III had to say. He was the leading candidate to cast the decisive vote.

Gay had never discussed the Anthony Amendment on the Senate floor, nor had he ever voted on it. He, like Pollock, was a new face, but NAWSA and NWP women in Louisiana knew he was under the "friendly influence" of Robert Ewing, the state's major newspaper publisher. For more than a month, NWP campaigners in Louisiana had been pursuing a pledge from him through a network of committees in every major population center. Despite his apparent negative attitude, the Louisiana women told reporters they were "still optimistic" that Gay would vote alongside the state's other senator, Joseph Ransdell.

Two days after the Senate defeat, Robert Ewing's Louisiana newspapers reported on a plan proposed by the state's assistant attorney general, Harry Gamble. He recommended reviving the Anthony Amendment with specific changes intended to address the concerns of states' rights senators.

Gamble was a staunch opponent of the federal amendment and, according to his son, a "segregationist up to the hilt." He had spent the previous year criticizing Louisiana's sole US senator who backed the Anthony Amendment. In a "Open Letter to the United States." Senator Ransdell," a lengthy legal brief that ran to more than 10,000 words, Gamble laid out his case that the Civil War "did not settle States' Rights" and that, were the Anthony Amendment to become part of the Constitution, it "would subject the South to the dangers of Negro suffrage." Now he proposed to break the deadlock in the Senate in the very way that Kate Gordon had recommended: by adding a Jim Crow-friendly carve out to the Anthony Amendment that would "pull it

"It might be a happy time," Gamble told the Shreveport Times, "to propose a compromise, which will give the women of the United States the vote by federal amendment, without granting the Congress the dangerous and totally unnecessary right to enforce it." The problem with the Anthony Amendment as written, he explained, was that "it gives Congress the privilege to enforce the right" of "negro women to vote in the South." Even worse, he warned, it "incidentally makes it the

Gamble made it apparent that he intended to propose the concept in Congress. "If the advocates of the present amendment are sincere," he said, "they will instantly accept the compromise."

Five days after Gamble's suggestion was reported in the Louisiana news, the Florida Federation of Women's Clubs' Department of Civil Service Reform chairman filed a complaint with the White House. "My dear Mr. Tumulty," wrote Florence Cooley on February 17, "this is the first day that the paper has not carried double-headed advertisements for the Democracy Prison Special. The automobile will arrive tomorrow, along with the specialized onslaught."

She was enraged by the National Woman's Party's three-week cross-country speaking tour, which included two dozen former Occoquan, District Workhouse, and District Jail inmates. Following the Senate's rejection of the Anthony Amendment, a group of ladies fled Washington. It made its first visit in Charleston and planned to finish its tour before the lame-duck session ended on March 4. The Prison Special had speaking engagements scheduled in Florida, Tennessee, Louisiana, Texas, California, Colorado, Illinois, Wisconsin, Massachusetts, and New York.

Tumulty had other concerns to attend, such as the parade he was organizing to celebrate Wilson's return to the US. He informed Wilson in Paris on his plans for a military procession led by the president. Initially, the plan was to do this in Washington, but Wilson, House, and Tumulty all agreed that starting in the "Democratic city of Boston" would be preferable. Not only would this guarantee a supportive crowd—the Boston mayor, Andrew Peters, had served in the Wilson administration for four years under McAdoo—but it was also in Senator Henry Cabot Lodge's backyard. Putting on a pro-Wilson show for the incoming head of the Foreign Relations Committee would send a message about the president's popularity and his proposal for a League of Nations.

On January 22, the Japanese delegation learned for the first time that Wilson intended to make ratification of the League Charter a requirement for signing the peace treaty. By then, Japan had paid little attention to the League. If it joined, anti-Asian prejudice would result in them being repeatedly outvoted by European nations and America. As a result, they focused on the conditions of the peace accord.

House developed a proposal with a preamble borrowed from the Declaration of Independence proclaiming that "all men are created equal." On February 10, the same day the U.S. As the Senate rejected the Anthony Amendment, he shared it with British Foreign Secretary Arthur Balfour.

The previous British prime minister, a Conservative in Lloyd George's coalition government, provided a caustic take on what House was up to. "Colonel House's view was that such a preamble, however little it squared with American practice, would appeal to American sentiment," he said in a concurrent memo. Meanwhile, "the rest of the formula" would avoid any implied promise to enable Japanese immigration. Balfour was concerned that vague abstractions like these could cause more harm than good by instilling "hopes in the Japanese public that could not be fulfilled," resulting in "perpetual controversy."

Britain's response convinced Wilson that using high-sounding rhetoric to cover up the issue would not work. The president immediately abandoned the notion, uninterested in giving anything substantive other than platitudes from the House and unwilling to dedicate any more attention to the topic.

However, the Japanese were serious about their race neutrality plan, and when they did not receive a response from the House, Japan's delegation publicly offered fresh text to Wilson's committee on February 13. According to their proposal, the League's charter would state that "equality of nations being a basic principle of the League of Nations," and that all League members would "as soon as possible" extend "to all alien nationals" within their states "equal and just treatment in every respect making no distinction, either in law or in fact, on account of their race or nationality."

Wilson personally called the idea "absurdly mild," but as chairman, he refused to support it. Doing so would have necessitated additional rounds of negotiations with Britain, France, and the majority of the other members of his committee, all of which would take time. He was now in grave danger of missing the end of the third and final session of Congress. The front page of the previous day's New York Times had previously warned, "Delays May Force Wilson to Sail Without League Plans"—an outcome that would frustrate his principal aim in coming to Washington, which was to present the Senate with his finished League of Nations plan.

The same day Japan made its formal presentation to his committee, Wilson proposed a vote to send the League charter to the full peace conference without the race neutrality provision. House attempted to persuade the Japanese that Britain, not America, rejected the initiative. The Japanese accepted defeat and decided to fight another day. The committee's vote to transmit the draft charter to the peace conference was unanimous.

Wilson was now free to board the USS George Washington and return to America, with the draft League charter in hand, which he did the next day. Racial equality would not be a guiding principle of the League of Nations or global peace.

Chapter 17: 'This Tardy Act of Justice'

Wilson had not stayed in Washington at the end of the 65th Congress. At noon on March 4, he was already at sea, on his way back to Paris. But, before leaving the country, he gave a speech in New York that predicted a lengthy departure. "I will not come back 'till it's over, over there,'" he proclaimed to his audience at the Metropolitan Opera House, quoting George M. Cohan's popular song. He would not return for more than three months.

In his haste to depart to Europe, Wilson left behind a dissatisfied new Senate majority. "52 Senators Lined Up Against League Plan," the New York Herald wrote on the morning of his departure. The skeptics were five Democrats and 47 Republicans, representing 54% of the newly elected Senate. The Constitution states that one vote from more than one-third of the Senate can defeat a treaty, implying that Wilson's League of Nations proposal was in severe difficulty and would fail if the senators' objections were not addressed.

The Chicago Tribune said Democratic Senate leaders, including Hitchcock, appeared to take the opposition of so many senators far more seriously than the president did.

Winston Churchill, Britain's secretary of state for air and war, observed a dramatic contrast between the president's willingness to defer to European interests and his refusal to deal with the Senate during the Paris peace talks. "The wide generosity which he vented upon Europe," Churchill wrote in his book The Aftermath, "ended pretty sharply at the shores of his own country. In every major choice, he was a cunning and brazen party politician.

Norris answered Wilson's charges with an open letter published in the Nebraska State Journal. "In the name of democracy and for the avowed purpose of making the world safe for democracy," the senator said of the president, "he went to Europe in a splendor and gorgeousness never equaled in the history of the world." Leaving behind the unfinished business of women's suffrage and the reconstruction of a nation still near completely on a war footing, while "his fellow citizens were sacrificing in every possible way," Wilson had behaved as if he were a "king, monarch or

Without a doubt, America needs emergency legislation to restore peacetime conditions and to free the country's farms, industry, transportation, finances, and civil rights from the administrative mandates of war. However, Congress could not even begin legislative hearings on these issues, let alone pass legislation, unless Wilson agreed to convene the freshly elected House and Senate. If Wilson's previous three-month absence had hampered Congress's ability to operate, holding its convening until his return from this second trip would preclude it from operating altogether.

Since 1789, the Constitution has designated December 1 of the year following the election as the first meeting of each newly elected Congress. That extended interregnum was necessary in the 18th century, when there were no telegraphs or railroads, and many elected officials had to travel to Washington for months. In fact, for the first hundred years of the nation's existence, the Senate was usually in session for less than half a year. By the twentieth century, however, the development of the federal government's responsibilities had rendered that unhurried arrangement completely impractical. And this year, in particular, the nation's pressing demands in the aftermath of World War made it critical for the new Congress to get to work as quickly as possible.

The president's ability to prohibit Congress from assembling had previously caused problems in American history. For years, calls for reform have grown. Less than three years from now, George Norris would write what would become the 20th Amendment, finally repealing the outdated provision of the Constitution that prevented Congress from meeting for more than a year after the election. The 20th Amendment would set the start date of each new Congress on January 3, just two months after election. Presidents would never be able to keep Congress from acting for political reasons again.

In the final minutes of the 65th Congress, as the president sailed eastward at eighteen knots toward the French port of Brest, Jeannette Rankin rose in the House of Representatives to deliver a brief farewell statement. Even before she spoke, the males around the hall applauded her.

Unlike Wilson's speech the night before in New York, her message conveyed neither defiance nor partisanship. Instead of running for reelection in the House, she ran for Senate and lost. Her vote against the war drew strong criticism, most of it personal, and was likely the cause of her fall. Nonetheless, she was full of admiration for her colleagues, Congress, and the opportunity to serve.

Those were nice words, and they were correct. The males of the House treated their first female colleague as an equal. She had many serious mentors, particularly Republican leader James Mann and Democratic candidate John Raker of California. Furthermore, during her first tenure, the House appointed her as the ranking member of the Committee on Woman Suffrage, an appointment based solely on merit given her vast expertise in suffrage activity, and no less an honor.

However, she was departing Congress with one big regret. "I am sorry to leave you before the women of this Nation are enfranchised," she said. Now she has bestowed upon the 66th Congress the duty and "great trust" of finally completing the task of many lifetimes.

"I love you, the Sixty-fifth Congress," she added earnestly, "and I shall never forget you."

Her concluding comments, delivered at the end of a Congress that had become violently split over the League of Nations, the president's extended relocation to Europe, and a thousand minor disagreements over how to deconstruct the federal superstructure left over from the war, were startlingly beautiful. Each of the men loved hearing them. They impulsively stood in ovation for their leaving colleague.

By the end of the lame-duck session, James Mann, the House minority leader who a little more than a year ago left his hospital bed at Johns Hopkins Hospital in Baltimore to cast a critical vote for the Anthony Amendment, was back on his feet and declared himself good as new. He was, however, not completely healthy, and his ailments had contributed to a disappointing campaign for speakership in the final days of the 65th Congress. After Republicans reclaimed control of the House, he should have been appointed minority leader.

Mann was also dealing with a family catastrophe. Last September, while he was periodically hospitalized, his only son, who was 28 and suffering from tuberculosis, committed suicide with a revolver. "I am pretty nearly all in, and I do not want to wait for the end of tuberculosis," his son stated in a note. As Mann continued to heal from bereavement and his own illness, he couldn't help but think about the fragility of life—and the need of returning to Congress to accomplish as much as he could, while he could.

The chairman-elect of the Woman Suffrage Committee, aware that he had taken on the "great trust" of finishing the task begun by Representative George Julian and Senator Samuel Pomeroy over fifty years ago, was eager to get started as soon as possible. The New York Times commented on Mann's decision to make the Susan B. Anthony Amendment "his one supreme legislative effort." Mann announced that "the Committee plans the introduction of the Susan B. Anthony Amendment immediately upon the convening of Congress, and an immediate favorable report of the amendment," and promised that he would then press for "the speedy passage of the amendment through the House."

Mann was powerless to intervene until the president convened Congress. Meanwhile, he was well aware that the longer Wilson waited, the more difficult it would be to secure adoption of the amendment in time for women to vote in the presidential election of 1920.

Thirty-six states must pass the Anthony Amendment before it can become part of the Constitution. However, the vast majority of state legislatures met only every other year, in an odd-numbered year. In the first quarter of 1919, forty-three state legislatures were in session. By April, all but two would have been adjourned. Worse, thirty-eight of the forty-three did not meet again until 1921. The Suffragists argued that Wilson's failure to assemble Congress was "criminally wasting" the opportunity for ratification.

Two hundred NWP women had demonstrated in New York on the eve of Wilson's departure to make this point. The message on one of their banners was: "We Demand That You Call an Extra Session of Congress Immediately to Pass the Suffrage Amendment." They stated that they were there "to express to President Wilson, on the eve of his sailing again for Europe, the grave indignation of American women that he should once more leave the country without having done his utmost for the enfranchisement of his country's womanhood."

Wilson was once again shielded from the banners the women carried with their American flag because, long before he emerged from the Metropolitan Opera House, they were roughed up by police, soldiers, and sailors who tore down their standards and frog-marched them to the police station, bruised and bleeding. Although the war had ended five months earlier, there was still antagonism against peaceful anti-Wilson demonstrations, just as there was in Boston.

Wilson's mood quickly deteriorated when he landed in Paris with the First Lady in mid-March. During his brief absence, Colonel House and the rest of the American delegation had not emphasized the League of Nations as he desired. There was a danger that the peace treaty and the League Covenant would be severed. "All to do over again," he complained to Edith as he set about ensuring that "the League of Nations should be made an integral part of the Treaty." He abandoned his long-standing routine of ample rest and relaxation, now working "at all hours of the night," remembered Lloyd George, who found it remarkable that Wilson would not take a break even as the "rest of us found time for golf and we took Sundays off."

At home, the call to convene the Congress grew louder, while the president tuned it out, immersed in the details of European demands for reparations and territory, each new claim implicitly or overtly offered in exchange for support for some component of his goal, the League. For a time, Wilson fought these numerous ideas that violated his Fourteen Points, and by the end of March, the Big Four—Lloyd George, Clemenceau, Orlando, and Wilson—were deadlocked.

April started on a bad note. The ongoing conflicts among the Big Four coincided with Wilson's illness from the influenza that had earlier affected Tumulty and House, and many others in Washington and Paris. Fever, congestion, and diarrhea kept him in bed for nearly a week. When he healed, he considered returning home, but not because of illness or to meet American demands that he handle critical domestic issues. Rather, Wilson's public contemplation about an impending departure on the USS George Washington indicated his willingness to withdraw from the negotiations if things didn't go his way.

Wilson gave up one sacrifice for the League. On April 11, Japanese members of Wilson's committee attempted yet again to include their racial equality proposal in the League Covenant. This time, they provided a significantly watered-down version. Instead of calling for each League member to treat foreign nationals "equally," the new phrase would just require "just" treatment.

Wilson rejected the plan, claiming that his "own interest, let me say, is to quiet discussion that raises national differences and racial prejudices." Wilson wished to keep the Japanese proposal out of the League's discussions. However, when a majority of his committee voted for it, he imposed a unanimity rule, effectively defeating it.

Three weeks later, on May 6, the Wall Street Journal reported rumors in banking circles that, despite the president's stated intentions, a special session of Congress "might be called before the end of the current month." The reason was the desperate need for appropriations to keep the government-run railroads operational. Even the banks were unaware that the government was experiencing additional concealed financial difficulties. For months, McAdoo's successor as treasury secretary, former House member Carter Glass, had been struggling to handle a cash flow situation that he understood could only be resolved through congressional appropriations.

Glass requested Wilson's permission to use the cash Congress had given to the commander in chief's discretion for war operations, but even that would only support the bureau's salary and costs until May 15. Wilson agreed, but refused to compromise on the extraordinary session. He specifically urged Glass not to prepare for "the calling of Congress by May."

However, when the May deadline approached, the nation's railroads, military personnel payments, and other critical government activities faced a severe budget shortfall. Without congressional appropriations, which are required by the Constitution to be granted each year, the treasury secretary could do nothing else to avert disaster. On May 7, Glass went public.

"The War Risk Bureau has reached its limit. The necessity for funds to sustain it has become so critical that this session is required," Glass told the press. He went on to say that, with the new fiscal year commencing on July 1 and no appropriations laws having passed, other measures to fund the rest of the government "are almost as vitally important."

Wilson issued a telegraph from Paris that same day, summoning a special session of Congress to begin Monday, May 19. Glass had suggested holding the extraordinary session "at the earliest possible moment," no later than May 15. The treasury secretary, visibly upset, told the New York Times that he had no idea why Wilson pushed the deadline out, and that "every delay would handicap the War Risk Bureau."

The president's request for a special session was clearly issued "much against his will but under the call of plain necessity," according to the Wall Street Journal. Nonetheless, "Congressional leaders of both parties were gratified the President had issued the call," the New York Times said. And, while the short-term financial issue will now be addressed, the top domestic priority remained clear. "It is generally accepted," claimed the Times, "that the Republicans will, almost as soon as Congress convenes, endeavor to force the suffrage amendment through the Senate." Representative James Mann would move even faster to pass the Anthony Amendment in the House.

The Wyoming gentleman, who was happy to claim he had always voted with women, renounced the award in favor of his Illinois colleague James Mann. The opportunity of introducing House Joint Resolution 1 on the first day of the session was granted to the previous House Republican leader, who is now chairman of the Woman Suffrage Committee. Mann's resolution was identical to the one filed in 1878 by Susan Anthony's friend Senator Aaron Sargent and most recently by the first woman in Congress, Representative Jeannette Rankin.

Mann moved with lightning speed after that. Never in American history has a constitutional amendment been introduced and passed so rapidly. Mann's committee approved the motion the next morning, even before the House got Wilson's cabled message to begin the session. From then on, he had support from the House's new leadership.

On the second day of the 66th Congress, only hours after James Mann reported the Anthony Amendment from the Woman Suffrage Committee to the floor, Majority Leader Mondell made an announcement that elicited applause from the entire chamber. The amendment would be voted on the following day. As promised, Mann took the floor on May 21, the third day of the session, and defeated parliamentary challenges, weakened minority amendments, and all demands for delays. As a result, by midafternoon, the Anthony Amendment had won a landslide of completely unexpected proportions.

The last man to speak in support of the amendment represented the first state to offer women the right to vote, fifty years ago. Frank Mondell put the day's momentous decision in context, commemorating the generations of now-deceased women who had made this success unavoidable, as well as those who, having "fought the good fight all these years," have lived to "now see the dawn of the day of final victory."

One of the legislators on both sides of the aisle who applauded Mondell's words had a unique purpose for doing so. Daniel Anthony Jr., a Republican from Kansas and the son and namesake of an anti-slavery pioneer, inherited his aunt Susan's goal. When he was born, she was fifty years old and was the Revolution's publisher. On this day, he was her living legacy in the Capitol, where she had fought so hard for this modest act of justice that would bear her name forever.

During a cross-country swing in April 1919, the Republican whip, future vice president Charles Curtis of Kansas, canvassed members of his party's caucus and publicly reported that the suffrage amendment would receive the necessary two-thirds vote in the Senate, despite the fact that not all senators had yet made their positions public. "I do not think there is a shadow of doubt as to its immediate passage," he stated at the time. His nose-counting was publicly acknowledged two weeks before the Senate voted on House Joint Resolution 1. By that point, sixty-six senators had publicly pledged their support, two more than was required.

Just as in the House, the election of a Republican majority led to complete changes in chairmanships and leadership positions, with suffrage supporters replacing opponents. On June 3, when the historic day arrived to consider the Anthony Amendment in the newly formed Senate, the man in the chair was President Pro Tem Albert Cummins, a long-time Anthony Amendment supporter who had hosted Sara Bard Field, Mabel Vernon, and other prominent NWP leaders in his Iowa home.

The opponents were not listening. The Senate debate lasted hours and into the next day, revealing once again why federally guaranteed voting rights for women had taken so long to acquire. Newly elected Senator Pat Harrison proposed the "white citizens" amendment, which had previously been proposed by his fellow Mississippi Democrat, John Sharp Williams. Williams himself took the opportunity to remind his colleagues that the 15th Amendment outlawing voter discrimination based on race was "a mistake." Ellison "Cotton Ed" Smith of South Carolina joined in warning that when a "man votes for the Susan B. Anthony Amendment, he votes to enfranchise the other half of that race." William Borah of Idaho, the lone Republican to vote for the "white citizens" amendment, opined that "nobody intends that the two and a half million

Nonetheless, each of these senators was aware that more than two-thirds of his colleagues were ready to vote for the Anthony Amendment. At the end of the debate, the white supremacist argument changed course. Senator Edward Gay of Louisiana stepped forward to present the new argument.

The roll call vote on Gay's amendment demonstrated how much had changed in the new Congress. Even Jones and Williams voted against the amendment they had just supported in the lame-duck session. The 77 percent majority to eliminate this final procedural hurdle meant that the Anthony Amendment had made it. The assembled senators, journalists, and spectators all knew they were about to see history.

Senator Cummins, in the chair, announced the vote on final passage: two-thirds plus two, as expected. Republicans supported the legislation 40-9; Democrats delivered a substantial majority, but it fell short of the required two-thirds, splitting 26-21. Leaders of both parties were understandably proud of their triumph.

The party didn't wait. It started right there on the Senate floor and in the galleries, with movie cameras waiting outside the Capitol. Normally, the presiding officer would call for order and threaten to clear the galleries if decorum was not restored. But Senator Cummins grinned and allowed the cheers and raucous ovation to continue, effectively halting Senate proceedings. Nearly a century and a half after Abigail Adams warned Congress that women "will not hold ourselves bound by any laws in which we have no voice or representation," men in Congress responded. Now, the Senate's business could, as Wilson put it, "afford a little while to wait."

Chapter 18: 'The Last Thing to Be Brought About'

AT THE MILLENNIUM, THE GALLUP organization polled the American population to identify the most significant event of the twentieth century. Sixty-six percent chose "Women gaining the right to vote" over putting a man on the moon, the collapse of the Soviet Union, World War I, and the Great Depression. Only World War II ranked higher.

To Woodrow Wilson in Paris, the final passage of the women's suffrage amendment in Congress on June 4, 1919, appeared far less crucial. In a mess of communications from Tumulty, it amounted to six words: "Suffrage Amendment passed Senate this afternoon."

Wilson's attention was drawn to the Senate mutiny over the peace treaty's secrecy. The 80,000-word document, which included 440 articles, maps, and charts, had previously been given to the German government for signature. Copies circulated freely in Germany. Despite the Fourteen Points' promise of "open covenants of peace, openly arrived at," and the Senate's constitutional advice-and-consent role, Wilson continued to oppose the senators' demands for a copy of the document.

Meanwhile, the fight to ratify the Anthony Amendment was begun. Its progress grabbed headlines practically every day. Only five state legislatures were still in session when Congress granted final approval on June 4, but within days, three of those five—Wisconsin, Michigan, and Illinois—voted to ratify. The amount grew as governors across the country, prompted by tremendous public support, called their legislatures into special session. By the conclusion of the first week of July, Kansas, Ohio, New York, Pennsylvania, Massachusetts, Texas, Iowa, and Missouri had all voted to incorporate women's voting rights into the Constitution.

Now that he was back on American soil, the line to speak with the president on domestic issues was long. But he had returned home with one main goal: to persuade the Senate to accept the treaty and the League of Nations covenant without changes or objections. Even before departing Europe, he had begun preparing a cross-country speaking tour to rally the public behind his campaign. Tumulty outlined a tentative itinerary to Wilson in a June 28 cable from Paris: "Return to Washington; address Congress. Spend two to three weeks in Washington, meeting with Senators and Congressmen and clearing up your desk. Tour the country, including the Pacific Coast, if feasible, to battle the Senate on the League of Nations."

On July 10, two days after arriving in Washington, the president addressed the Senate, urging them to approve the League and the treaty. By that time, the document had been finalized and signed by Germany and thirty-one other countries, making amendments very difficult. The senators had yet to get an official copy, so he carried one to the Capitol. "I avail myself of the earliest opportunity to lay the treaty before you," he said at the start of his speech, without irony.

Back at the White House, Wilson had a large list of non-treaty issues vying for his attention. The country was in deep recession due to roaring inflation, railway and steel strikes loomed, and an epidemic of lynchings continued to scandalize the nation, fueled by a contemporary Ku Klux Klan resurrected by The Birth of a Nation.

During the summer of 1919, there were more than twenty major race riots across the country. Each began with white-on-black violence. Much of the hatred fueling the mayhem stemmed from Wilson's own policies. One of the worst riots occurred in the heavily segregated federal city of Washington, D.C., when a drunken mob of over a hundred uniformed soldiers, sailors, and Marines, some recently discharged veterans and some on active duty, launched a vigilante attack on Charles Ralls, a Black man they suspected of harassing a white woman and stealing her umbrella the night before.

Throughout the boiling violence, Wilson remained absolutely detached. He left town Friday for a weekend sail on the Mayflower. He carried no papers with him and made it clear that he would not be disturbed. The White House and the Navy Department had no communication with the president's party from the moment it left until it returned on Monday morning. "It was presumed," the Associated Press wrote, "that the President was enjoying a complete rest."

Wilson did not address the rising violence when he returned from his cruise Monday, citing stomach problems and diarrhea. On the fourth day of unrest, he resumed work but emphasized League meetings. Pastors from Washington churches, together with the National Race Congress, signed an open letter urging the president to establish "a competent and efficient police department" to safeguard "law-abiding colored citizens" from "extreme lawlessness" in the federal city. Wilson made no comment.

Secretary of War Newton Baker was ultimately granted a brief meeting on Tuesday afternoon, giving the president enough time to merely state that he would defer to Baker's decision. Baker promptly dispatched 2,000 troops to the capital, but the delayed military and law police reaction required the assistance of a summer storm at the end of the week to halt the violence, which had already killed nearly forty people in the capital.

Soon after Washington was calmed, riots broke out in Chicago, killing thirty-eight persons, both black and white, during the next week. As race riots erupted in city after city during what became known as the Red Summer, the call for a presidential statement grew louder. Wilson still did not say anything. The inspiring, imaginative words he had mustered for other occasions may have served as a soothing salve for the nation's gaping wounds from racial war. But privately, he admitted he didn't know what to say.

Grayson's medical reports to the press during the Washington riots indicated food poisoning. However, Wilson had a long medical history of gastrointestinal issues, of which his doctor was fully aware. His indigestion was the result of a series of chronic illnesses that had accumulated during his life. He has suffered headaches since he was a youngster. He most likely had a small stroke when he was thirty-nine. He was diagnosed with arteriosclerosis at age 49. Grayson noted evidence of kidney impairment during Wilson's first term. By the time Wilson began his second term in the White House, twenty years of hypertension and degenerative cerebrovascular disease had taken their toll.

Robert Lansing, the career diplomat and secretary of state whom the president largely ignored at the peace conference, advised Wilson to "not lose a moment in coming to an agreement with the mild reservationists,' who were now in the mood to compromise on reasonable terms." However, the president rejected all friendly conciliatory advice. He said he intends to force the Senate to "take its medicine." When the French ambassador assured Wilson that both France and Britain would accept the reservations Republicans were discussing, the president brusquely replied that he would "consent to nothing." Colonel House advised the president "that a fight was the last thing to be brought about." In response, Wilson severed ties with House, refusing to see his friend and closest adviser again.

In reality, the vast majority of treaty backers supported compromise. Reservations, unlike amendments, would not necessitate the opening of the treaty to renegotiation, which had been Wilson's strongest argument for senators to accept it "as is." There were enough of the so-called mild reservationists in the Senate that, if Wilson were willing to accommodate their concerns, he would be virtually certain of winning both treaty ratification and American participation in the League.

For a brief period in the weeks following his return to America, Wilson gave the Anthony Amendment some presidential attention. He directed Tumulty to send presidential telegrams of one or two phrases each to Alabama, Georgia, Virginia, and Kentucky. But by the time the presidential train arrived at its first stop, news had spread that two of those states, Alabama and Virginia, had already ignored the telegrams and rejected the amendment.

It was now early September. Fourteen states had approved the Anthony Amendment, all without presidential intervention. However, twenty-two more were needed. A survey of state legislatures found twenty-four states had legislative majorities in favor of the amendment. Unfortunately, only three of them were planned to meet regularly before 1921. The urgent aim was to persuade governors to hold special meetings. Even the president's one-sentence telegrams may have helped with this. However, there will be no more of those telegrams in 1919.

Along with Wilson's diplomatic tour, advocates of the Anthony Amendment rallied legislators in state capitals across the country. On September 9, while movie cameras and a conga line of cars packed with reporters accompanied Wilson's march through Bismarck, North

Dakota, legislators in New Hampshire chose to make their state the sixteenth to ratify.

The Mayflower landed in Los Angeles at 9:00 a.m. On September 20, the president was still sleeping. He had been suffering headaches for days. Grayson quickly escorted him to his downtown hotel, where he slept until midday before waking him for the regular parade around the city streets, with the same pageantry at each stop. The president returned to the hotel and rested until six o'clock. He went right back to bed after giving a speech to a welcoming audience at the Shrine Auditorium that evening.

Late that night on the Mayflower, Wilson had his worst asthmatic attack of the voyage. His facial muscles jerked, and he felt nauseated. He felt like he couldn't catch his breath. Tumulty canceled the remaining addresses in Kansas, Oklahoma, Arkansas, and Tennessee, per Grayson's directions. The presidential special was rerouted back to Washington, where Wilson died one week later from a major stroke.

His left arm and leg were immobile, the left half of his face drooped, and his digestive issues had worsened, indicating stroke damage to his central nervous system. Weakness in the muscles on the left side of his tongue, mouth, and pharynx made swallowing difficult and hampered communication. His right eye's vision had been affected by a previous stroke; now his left eye's vision was compromised. He had periodic double vision and frequent dizzy spells. He couldn't read, sit in a chair to eat, or sign his name. His muscles were weak, and his memory was defective. White House Chief Usher Ike Hoover described him as "mentally but a geyser"—a pretender—"compared to the normal understanding of his great mind."

Edith, Grayson, and Tumulty went to great measures to conceal the severity of the president's handicap. Wilson remained in seclusion for more than four months, and the government effectively ran itself.

"He has been ill since last October," Wilson's press secretary at Versailles, Ray Stannard Baker, wrote in his notebook in late January 1920, "and he has no idea what is going on. He receives little direct news and rarely interacts with others. Was there ever such a circumstance in our history?"

By March, after months of debating the wording of so-called moderate reservations to the treaty and the League covenant, the Senate had reached a provisional accord that just needed Wilson's approval. Ray Baker appealed with Edith to persuade the president to "set aside the trivialities" and join the Senate in establishing a League and doing so swiftly. He would have everyone with him in such a move." Baker said the president faced a choice between accepting "merely inconsequential changes—or getting no treaty and League." Writing in his diary, Baker despaired: "Yet [the president] hardens at any such suggestion: the very moment of yielding anything to the Senate appears to drive him into stubborn immovability."

Telegrams were mostly ineffective anyway. Since March, when Washington's passage brought the Anthony Amendment within one state of the required thirty-six, no other state legislature has stepped up to complete the job. So when the Tennessee Senate approved it on August 13, suffrage supporters across the country were ecstatic. The possibilities for winning in the state's House of Representatives were enticing: a roll call on a preliminary procedural matter resulted in an exact tie, 48-48.

Speaker of the House Seth L. Walker, a Democrat, was opposed to the Anthony Amendment. If he could be persuaded to change his vote, the struggle would be won, and the Democrats could take credit for pushing it over the top. Tumulty contacted Walker on Wilson's behalf, per Carrie Chapman Catt's request. The one-sentence letter urged his support for ratification "in the interest of national harmony." However, the Speaker immediately responded to Wilson's telegram with his own, warning the president that he would not "surrender honest convictions for political expediency or harmony."

On the day of the final vote, another Tennessee House member showed willingness to tip the balance. Republican Harry Burn, unlike most of his colleagues, had remained undecided, but in the procedural voting thus far, he had agreed with the majority mood in his constituency, opposing the Anthony Amendment. During the final balloting, a page on the House floor brought him a note. He opened it right before he voted. The letter came from his widowed mother, not the White House.

In theory, 30 million eligible American women could now vote. According to the 1920 census, that included 10% who were "Negro, Indian, Chinese, Japanese," or "other." However, Wilson's new attorney general, A. Mitchell Palmer, the former chairman of the House Democratic Caucus who co authored the Shafroth-Palmer amendment in 1914, was just as concerned as the president with enforcing minority voting rights. In November, he adopted the same hands-off approach to abuses of non-white women's rights that the Wilson Justice Department had routinely used for men.

Nationally, many Black women were able to vote in November. The Washington Post voiced doubts that they could understand the complexities of voting, but was concerned that if they did in Maryland, they would have a significant impact. "If the colored women, of whom 30,000 are registered in the State, can master the ballot (and they are all Republicans) Harding will get a record vote," the newspaper projected. "Half of this number can be spared and he will still have a decisive majority."

Woodrow Wilson, unable to leave the White House, voted by mail from New Jersey. Months before, he dubbed the poll a "great and solemn referendum" on the League of Nations. According to the Chicago Tribune, he was now "obsessed" with his "popular vindication at the polls," and those close to him were concerned that a Democratic loss "would not only shock him severely but produce disastrous effects upon his mental and physical condition."

With no opinion polls to prepare him for the worst, the president must have been surprised by the scale of the Republican tsunami. In the largest popular vote landslide in a century, Ohio Senator Warren Harding and Massachusetts Governor Calvin Coolidge defeated the Democratic ticket of Ohio Governor James Cox and Wilson's Assistant Secretary of the Navy, Franklin D. Roosevelt. The Republican ticket achieved a record not only in terms of overall votes (inflated by millions of new female voters), but also in terms of victory margin (more than 26 percent). No presidential candidate has won so easily since James Monroe in 1820, when he ran nearly unopposed. It was also a rout in the electoral college. The Democratic candidates failed to carry a single state outside of the Solid South, let alone all of them.

In the run-up to the 1922 congressional elections, he endeavored to maintain contact with Cordell Hull, the Tennessee congressman who had helped implement the income tax during Wilson's first term and now led the Democratic National Committee. In one of their conversations, Wilson inquired about the influence of women's votes in the forthcoming midterm elections.

Printed in Dunstable, United Kingdom

75062492R00085